Mountain Biking
the Appalachians

Northwest
North Carolina

Southwest
Virginia

MOUNTAIN BIKING
THE APPALACHIANS

Northwest North Carolina
Southwest Virginia

Lori Finley

Thomas Horsch

John F. Blair, Publisher
Winston-Salem, North Carolina

Second Edition

BOOK DESIGN BY DEBRA LONG HAMPTON
MAPS BY THE ROBERTS GROUP AND LIZA LANGRALL
PHOTOS BY THE AUTHORS UNLESS OTHERWISE NOTED
COVER PHOTOGRAPH BY DENNIS COELLO
PRINTED AND BOUND BY R. R. DONNELLEY & SONS

Library of Congress Cataloging-In-Publication Data

Finley, Lori, 1958–
    Mountain biking the Appalachians. Northwest North Carolina/
southwest Virginia / Lori Finley, Thomas Horsch.
        p.   cm.
    Inlcudes index.
    ISBN 0-89587-205-6 (alk. paper)
    1. All terrain cycling—North Carolina—Guidebooks. 2. All terrian
cycling—Virginia—Guidebooks. 3. North Carolina—Guidebooks.
4. Virginia—Guidebooks. I. Horsch, Thomas, 1960– . II. Title.
GV1045.5.N75F56   1998
917.56'80443—dc21   98-5099

For Fred and Sandra
—Lori Finley

For my father, Robert Horsch. Let's ride.
—Thomas Horsch

Locator Map for Trail Rides

1. Junaluska Road Ride
2. Boone's Greenway Trail
3. Watauga River Road Ride
4. Sugar Mountain Trail Loop
5. Lower China Creek Loop
6. Yancey Ridge Loop
7. Roseborough to Globe Ride
8. Lower Wilson Ridge Trail
9. Upper Wilson Ridge Trail
10. Eighteen Mile Road Ride
11. Linville Gorge Loop
12. Wiseman's View Ride
13. Table Rock Loop
14. Benson Hollow Loop

15. Spencer Branch Loop
16. Barton Gap Loop
17. Old 84–Flat Top Loop
18. Jerry's Creek/Rowland Creek Trail
19. Whitetop Mountain Ride
20. Skulls Gap/Iron Mountain Loop
21. Skulls Gap Ride
22. Beartree Gap/Iron Mountain Trail Loop
23. Virginia Highlands Mountain Bike Challenge Course
24. Rush Trail/Chestnut Ridge Ride
25. Feathercamp Ridge Ride
26. Iron Mountain Trail to Damascus
27. Mock Holler Loop
28. Taylors Valley Loop
29. Virginia Creeper Trail: Damascus to Abingdon
30. Virginia Creeper Trail: Whitetop Gap to Damascus
31. New River Trail: Pulaski to Barren Springs
32. New River Trail: Foster Falls to Galax
33. New River Trail: Galax to Fries

Area Shown in Detail

VIRGINIA

NORTH CAROLINA

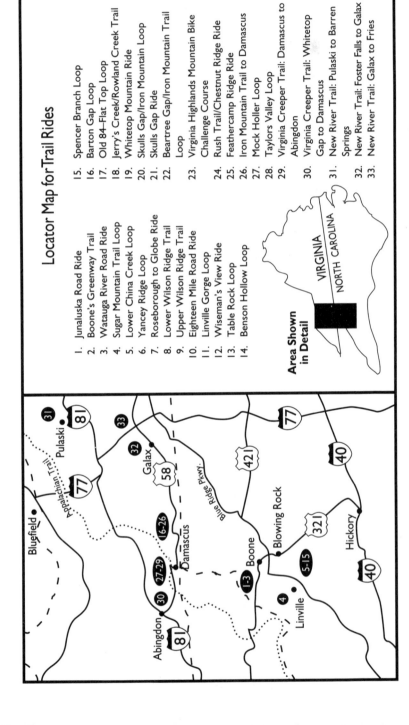

Contents

Rail Trails

Acknowledgments

I would like to extend my sincere appreciation to several people who helped in one way or another in the revision of this book.

I would like to thank Craig Franz of Linville, who guided me in the North Carolina section day after day, offered many suggestions for rides, always carried the maps, and knew where all the bad dogs lived. Without his help, I would still be wandering endlessly in the woods of Wilson Creek. We have many rides ahead of us, my friend. Watch those log crossings.

Tim Eling, Bob McKinney, and the rest of the staff and volunteers of the United States Forest Service/Mount Rogers National Recreation Area were invaluable resources for trail information, maps, and general suggestions about the rides in southwest Virginia. Keep those trails open, guys!

Bob and Steve Cheers from Mountain Sports, Ltd. in Bristol, kept my bike wheels spinning, even when I needed those last-minute emergency repairs and parts. Also, thanks to the staff of Piney Flats Bicycles in Piney Flats, Tennessee, and Highlands Ski and Outdoor Center in Abingdon, Virginia, for their support, advice, and feedback. Peter Elliot of K2 (Proflex) Bikes made sure I got that extra special attention and a quick response to my technical questions. Thanks go to Amy Smith at Trail Town Maps in Damascus for providing great trail maps of that area.

In the Boone area, I received help from several people, including Bob Wright, Bill Presley at Boone Bike and Touring, Mike Boone at Magic Cycles, and the kind folks at Blue Planet Map Company, who assisted with maps and trail information.

Trails don't just happen; they are built, mapped, maintained, and blazed. Through their sweat and the time they invest, several groups make it possible to ride the numerous single tracks of our area. The Virginia Creeper Trail Club, Iron Mountain

Trail Club, High Country Mountain Bike Association, and the International Mountain Bicycling Association are but a few of these organizations. Get involved with one of these, or a group like it, if you want to continue to see the trails remain open to mountain bikes. It really does make a difference.

Mountain-bike folks are the friendliest people on earth, and several of these friendly people have ridden with me during the course of this revision. Teddy Helton, David Morrison, Ed Craig, Sam and Elon, Bob Wright, R.D. Daniels, Bruce and Mary Morrison, Bill Devendorf, Walt Scarborough, and Chris Howard all kept me company along my journeys. Our trails will cross again; soon, I hope.

There are two people who encouraged me during this whole process that deserve a special thank you. Phoebe Cartwright of Blue Blaze Bike & Shuttle gave me rides, motherly advice, food, and porch time listening to stories of my adventures between shuttle runs. She is one of the few people I know that has trails and bikes on her mind as much as I do. Christy Parker, who helped me edit many of the rides, was always there to offer business advice and spiritual guidance. Thanks, buddy.

Lastly, I would like to thank the people at John F. Blair, Publisher, for giving me this opportunity to get paid for something I love to do. I probably would have done it for free!

Thomas Horsch

Many people helped me in the research and riding required for this book, and to them all I offer a hearty word of thanks.

First, I would like to thank Sarah and Mike Boone, owners of Magic Cycles in Boone, North Carolina. They eagerly told me about the area's classic mountain-bike rides and then spent quite a bit of time guiding me on the trails. I had a great time getting to know both of these good people while pedaling through the forests, and I appreciate everything they did to help me.

I also want to thank the staff of Rock & Roll Sports in Boone, who spent a considerable chunk of time in the back of the store tracing rides on maps. A few of the customers in the store, including John Holder, even took the time to tell me about a favorite ride or two. The staff of Blue Planet Map Company, including Mark Stroud, was quite helpful when I began the research for this book and always quickly mailed topographical maps to me when I needed them.

A word of thanks is also due Byrum Geisler, Kim Schmidinger, the staff of the Map Shop in Greenville, South Carolina, and Dennis Barnes of Denny's Stop & Go in Barren Springs, Virginia.

A special word of thanks goes to Jo Jo and Woody Keen of Blowing Rock, North Carolina, for literally going the extra mile to help me. I want to thank them for the hours spent trail riding, for the miles of dirt roads driven, and for their open-door hospitality.

Countless federal, state, and county employees helped me obtain accurate trail information. These people were always friendly, helpful, and brimming with quick answers to my questions. I particularly want to thank Phil Kromer of Pisgah National Forest's Grandfather District. A good friend to the High Country Mountain Bike Association, Phil took the time to answer all of my questions and to provide me with accurate information on trails in his district. I also want to thank Judy Johnson at New River Trail State Park for the mad faxing and for all her help.

Thanks to Angie and Roy Costner for taking care of my sweet daughters on the many occasions when my friends and I drove off at the crack of dawn in cars laden with mountain bikes.

And to my friends who have been with me on the trails for years now, I offer my heartfelt thanks. Sandra Thomas, Fred Thomas, Jim Sinclair, Brenda Cox, Herb Clark, and Owen Riley have stuck with me during the good times as well as the occasional bad. Despite enduring shuttle rides from hell, riding tortuous exploratory loops that took us to points unknown, and flirting with dusk because I wanted to check out one more "quick" ride, these good friends always rejoined me on the trails whenever I asked. Thanks for the help and the good memories. Years from now, these times will be my "good old days."

And finally, a special word of thanks goes to my family—Bob, Erin, and Elizabeth—for their support, encouragement, and pride. I couldn't have done it without you.

Lori Finley

The publisher would like to thank Eric Hougland, Tony Bentley, and Lanny Sparks.

Introduction

Imagine the sounds of a mountain creek singing off in the distance, the call of a red-tailed hawk, and the rustle of dry leaves skittering across a narrow trail. Think of the warm smell of a grassy meadow, the sweet fragrance of mountain magnolia blossoms, and the scent of high-elevation fir trees, calling up memories of Christmas morning. Picture a sun-drenched dirt road, a springtime hardwood forest exploding into a thousand shades of green, and a snow-encrusted mountain bald sparkling under a clear winter sky.

When you have summoned all of these to mind, you will have imagined the setting for some of the finest riding in the country. Welcome to mountain biking in the Appalachians.

The high country of northwest North Carolina and southwest Virginia is laced with a labyrinth of single-track trails, logging roads, and overgrown jeep tracks that beckon mountain bikers. For every route pedaled, there are a dozen more within a stone's throw, just waiting to be discovered. In fact, there are enough miles of designated trails and dirt roads that a cyclist could quit his job and easily spend a year or so exploring. But for the weekend warrior who doesn't have the luxury of full-time exploration, this guide features some of the classic rides of the region.

The 33 rides covered here will appeal to cyclists of diverse ability, experience, and even mood. Some trails hug the banks of low-lying rivers, while others climb into deep, hidden pockets of dense forest high in the hills. Ridden as loops, out-and-backs, and one-way shuttle rides, they range in difficulty from easy to strenuous, and in length from about 4 miles to about 50 miles.

With all these rides have to offer, you would expect to find crowds galore and wall-to-wall Lycra and titanium on any given weekend. But for whatever reason, these trails and roads have remained virtually undiscovered.

Pick up any mountain-bike magazine and you are sure to find its pages splattered with places like Moab and Crested Butte. Even North Carolina's Tsali trails have been featured. But have you read about the lofty Mount Rogers area in Virginia? How about the New River Trail? Have you even heard of North Carolina's Wilson Creek? Probably not, though outstanding mountain-biking opportunities abound in these areas.

"If the nearest town to Wilson Creek was San Francisco instead of Linville and Blowing Rock, its trails would be as known nationally as those in Marin," writes Dennis Coello in a *Bike* magazine article featuring unacclaimed cycling haunts. It's true. It's also true that many of these sites are relatively young. For example, the Mount Rogers area was established in the mid-1960s. And the rail trails described are part of a recent movement to convert abandoned railway corridors into multiuse recreation areas.

Though these spots are virtually crowd-free for now, enjoy the solitude while you can. Mountain biking this good will not remain untouched by fame for long.

Planning a Trip

Location

Half the mountain-bike rides in this guidebook are located in northwest North Carolina, near the towns of Boone and Blowing Rock. The other half are located in southwest Virginia, the majority in Mount Rogers National Recreation Area.

Routes

The routes described in this guidebook are grouped according to their location. Most can be completed in a day, many in half a day. Longer rides, such as the Linville Gorge Loop and the Virginia Creeper Trail, can be split up into several days by making lodging arrangements at points along the way in advance.

Before You Go

Before riding, it is advisable to check with the appropriate land administrators—the United States Forest Service, state parks, city parks, etc.—to confirm that the ride is open for mountain-bike use. At the time of this writing, all the routes covered were open to mountain bikers. But as we all know, a cloud of land-use controversy hangs over many mountain-biking areas. Land status is in a constant state of flux, and designations do change. You are ultimately responsible for ensuring that a trail is legal for pedaling. If you arrive at a trailhead and find that a No Mountain Biking sign has been posted, heed it. There are always plenty of other rides nearby.

Seasons

Because of the relatively mild winters in northwest North Carolina and southwest Virginia, most of these trails can be ridden year-round. Occasionally, they will be covered by snow or ice, particularly at the higher elevations. Some trails require river or creek crossings and should be avoided during cold weather, due to the risk of hypothermia. There are also some trails that should be avoided after periods of heavy rain, because of muddy conditions. These special considerations are noted in the individual ride descriptions. Mountain showers can be expected almost every day during the summer and are often a welcome, cooling relief from the heat. Hunting is permitted in some of the areas covered; mountain bikers are advised to wear fluorescent orange or some other bright, unnatural color.

Equipment and Essentials

Bicycle

A mountain bike with fat, knobby tires is necessary for most of these rides. Some trails are not technically challenging and can be ridden with either a full-fledged mountain bike or an all-terrain bicycle; this is noted in the individual ride descriptions.

Cyclocomputer

A cyclocomputer will make the directions in this book easier to follow, as turns and special features are noted to the tenth of a mile. Where possible, special features or landmarks at trail turnoffs have been noted for the benefit of cyclists without computers. You can complete these rides without a computer, but the chances of getting lost or missing a side trail to a waterfall or other highlight will be increased. Variations in tire pressure, in tire size, in cyclists' weight, and in individual cyclocomputers can produce different mileage readings over identical paths. Your readings may not always agree with those provided in this book, but they should be close.

Tool Kit

Many of these trails and roads wind through remote areas of forest, so a tool kit is highly recommended. The most common mechanical problem on the trail is a flat tire. Be certain you have a bicycle pump, tire irons, and a patch kit or a spare tube with you. If you have never changed a flat tire, learn how and practice at home before your ride. And if you are mechanically inept, bring along a friend who knows what a chain rivet tool and an Allen wrench are and, better yet, knows how to use them. Even a broken derailleur doesn't necessarily mean hoofing it back to the car; the right tool and a little ingenuity can have you up and spinning again, even though you will be limited to a single gear.

First-aid Kit

Again, many of these trails and roads are in remote sections of forest where the rescue index is poor. Bring a small, well-appointed first-aid kit with you. It is also a good idea to include a stubby candle and matches in the kit. In winter, you would not want to leave an injured rider without a warming fire while you sought medical assistance.

Water

When it comes to water, here are two pieces of advice: Bring your own, and bring enough. The creeks and rivers may look pristine, but gone are the days when cyclists could dip their water bottles into a cold mountain stream for an easy refill. There are some bad bugs around, the most notable being giardia. This single-cell organism can wreak havoc in your intestines if allowed to set up residence. So how much should you bring? You know your needs better than anyone else, but take a minimum of two water bottles. For long, strenuous rides or hot-weather rides, you'll need more. Sure, extra water adds weight, but staying well hydrated is of critical importance.

Safety

The United States Forest Service makes the following recommendations for safety in the back country:

1. Always let someone know where you are going, what route you are taking, when you expect to return, and what to do if you don't.
2. Check the weather forecast; be prepared with proper clothing and equipment for all potential weather conditions.
3. Don't push yourself beyond your limits.
4. Keep an eye on each other.
5. Plot your progress on a map as you travel; know where you are at all times.

Etiquette

Mountain bikers are the new kids on the block, or rather the new kids in the woods. We must be cognizant of the rights of others in the forest and treat others with courtesy. It takes only a few discourteous, irresponsible acts of destructive riding to close a trail to mountain bikes permanently. Ride responsibly. The National Off Road Bicycle Association (NORBA) promotes the following guidelines:

1. Yield the right of way to other nonmotorized recreationists;

realize that people judge all cyclists by your actions.

2. Slow down and use caution when approaching or overtaking others, and make your presence known well in advance.

3. Maintain control of your speed at all times, and approach turns in anticipation of someone around the bend.

4. Stay on designated trails to avoid trampling native vegetation, and minimize potential erosion by not using muddy trails or short-cutting switchbacks.

5. Do not disturb wildlife or livestock.

6. Do not litter; pack out what you pack in, and pack out more than your share whenever possible.

7. Respect public and private property, including trail-use signs and No Trespassing signs; leave gates as you found them.

8. Be self-sufficient, and let your destination and speed be determined by your ability, your equipment, the terrain, and present and potential weather conditions.

9. Do not travel solo when "bikepacking" in remote areas; leave word of your destination and when you plan to return.

10. Observe the practice of minimum-impact bicycling by "taking only pictures and memories and leaving only waffle prints."

11. Always wear a helmet whenever you ride.

Many of the trails covered in this guide are also used by equestrians, so exercise courtesy when you encounter horses. Always dismount and give the horse the right of way. If you approach the horse from the front, dismount and stand on the side of the trail. Stay in the horse's line of vision; wait to remount until it has moved well away. If you approach a horse from the rear, dismount and walk slowly until the rider notices you. The rider should move off the trail to allow you to walk your bike past. Remount when you are well away from the horse. If the rider doesn't move off the trail, ask him how he would like you to pass so that you won't spook his horse.

Campgrounds and Accommodations

Northwest North Carolina

The following campgrounds are managed by the Grandfather District of Pisgah National Forest:

1. Boone Fork Campground (no showers)
2. Curtis Creek Campground (no showers)
3. Mortimer Campground (no showers)

For campground information, maps, and current trail information, contact

United States Forest Service
Grandfather District, Pisgah National Forest
Route 1, Box 110A
Nebo, NC 28761
(704) 652-2144

A complete listing of campgrounds, accommodations, and bike shops for the northwest North Carolina area is available through the following offices:

Boone Chamber of Commerce
208 Howard Street
Boone, N.C. 28607
(704) 264-2225

Blowing Rock Chamber of Commerce
P.O. Box 406
Blowing Rock, N.C. 28605
(704) 295-7851

Banner Elk/Linville Chamber of Commerce
P.O. Box 335
Banner Elk, N.C. 28604
(704) 898-5605

Southwest Virginia

The following campgrounds are managed by Mount Rogers National Recreation Area:

1. Beartree Campground (hot showers)
2. Grindstone Campground (hot showers)
3. Hurricane Campground (hot showers)
4. Raccoon Branch Campground (no showers)
5. Raven Cliff Campground (no showers)
6. Comer's Rock Campground (no showers)
7. New River Campground (no showers)

For campground information, maps, and current trail information, contact

Mount Rogers National Recreation Area
3714 Highway 16
Marion, Va. 24354
(540) 783-5196

A complete listing of campgrounds, accommodations, and bike shops for the southwest Virginia area is available through the following offices:

New River Trail State Park
Route 2, Box 126F
Foster Falls, VA 24360
(540) 699-6778

Virginia Department of Conservation and Recreation
203 Governor Street, Suite 302
Richmond, Va. 23219
(804) 786-1712

Pulaski Chamber of Commerce
P.O. Box 169
Pulaski, Va. 24301
(540) 980-1991

Galax Chamber of Commerce
405 North Main Street
Galax, Va. 24333
(540) 236-2184

Washington County Chamber of Commerce
179 East Main Street
Abingdon, Va. 24210
(540) 628-8141

Publisher's Note

To help with the revisions for this second edition of *Mountain Biking the Appalachians: Northwest North Carolina/Southwest Virginia*, John F. Blair, Publisher, has enlisted the able assistance of Thomas Horsch. Thomas lives in Damascus, Virginia, where he is the current president of the Virginia Creeper Trail Club. He is also on the Board of Directors of the Iron Mountain Trail Club. He maintains a website at www.naxs.com/people/thorsch, which has more information about southwestern Virginia.

Although efforts have been made to insure the accuracy of the directions in this book, there are several important factors that should be taken into account. First of all, North Carolina's Department of Transportation has been slowly paving more and more of its dirt and gravel roads. Although a road might be dirt when this book goes to press, a few months later it might be paved. If you wish to avoid biking on paved roads, you might check with local bike shops to see if road conditions have changed since the book's publication.

Because some of these routes travel through national forests, it is important to remember that these areas may not have directional road signs. We have tried to offer landmarks for turnoffs, but keep in mind that single tracks that are obvious in the winter might disappear in the summer foliage. If you are going into national-forest areas, we advise you to take appropriate topographical maps, a compass, and a cyclocomputer. Without these devices, it is very possible that you will miss a turn and find yourself lost in the woods.

It is also important to remember that areas are constantly being opened and closed to mountain biking. If you discover that an area described in the book is closed to mountain bikers, we would appreciate hearing about it so we can make the necessary corrections in future printings.

Because calibrations on cyclocomputers can vary, you might also find that mileage information may be slightly different from your own calculations. However, if you find a glaring problem or omission with any of the directions, we would like to hear about that as well. Please call us at 1-800-222-9796, fax us at 336-768-9194, or email us at blairpub@aol.com.

The staff of John F. Blair, Publisher

Northwest North Carolina

Boone / Blowing Rock Area

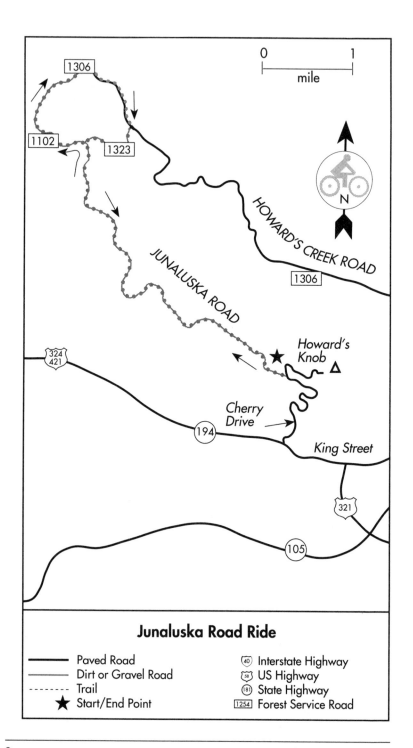

Junaluska Road Ride

———	Paved Road	40 Interstate Highway
~~	Dirt or Gravel Road	58 US Highway
- - - - -	Trail	181 State Highway
★	Start/End Point	1254 Forest Service Road

Junaluska Road Ride

Distance: 14 miles

Difficulty: Moderate

Riding surface: Dirt road

Maps: 1. Boone/Watauga County Map
2. USGS 7.5 minute quadrangle, Zionville, N.C.
3. USGS 7.5 minute quadrangle, Boone, N.C.

Access: From the intersection of U.S. 321 and U.S. 421 in Boone (at the historic Dan'l Boone Inn), proceed north on the combined U.S. 321/421 for about 0.1 mile. Just past the stone Advent Christian Church, turn right onto Cherry Drive. Follow the signs for Howard's Knob Park through a winding residential area. At 0.2 mile, you will come to a fork in the road; bear right onto Eastbrook Drive. Almost immediately, you will have to bear left to stay on Eastbrook Drive. At 0.4 mile, you will come to a yield sign and a wide Y-intersection; turn right onto Hunting Road. At 0.5 mile, turn left onto Eastview Drive. Hunting Road turns right. A short distance later, Eastview Drive continues up-hill to the right as Bear Trail Road goes to the left. At 1.0 mile, East Junaluska Road is on the left; continue straight. At 1.4 miles, park at the pull-off near the turnoff for Junaluska Road (S.R. 1102), now a hard-packed dirt-and-gravel road.

Elevation change: The ride begins at an elevation of 4,000 feet at the Junaluska Road turnoff. The elevation gain is steady but moderate, with the ride reaching a maximum of 4,300 feet at Trivett Gap. It drops to 3,800 feet, then quickly gains 400 feet on Curly Maple Road (S.R. 1323). On the return trip, there is a climb to 4,300 feet and then a gradual descent back to the 4,000-foot elevation at the end of the ride. The total elevation gain is 1,200 feet.

Configuration: Out-and-back

Sticking to hard-packed dirt-and-gravel roads for all but 1.3 miles of its 14-mile distance, this ride doesn't challenge cyclists with gnarly, technical single-track sections. However, it will give your heart and lungs a run for their money. And if your quad muscles aren't screaming at you at the top of the climbs, then you must have cheated and gotten a sag ride to the top.

Boone-area mountain bikers frequently train on Junaluska Road for two reasons: its physical challenge and its proximity to town. There are steady, long climbs followed by swift descents that barely give you enough time to catch your breath. There are also moderate stretches that offer you the chance for some gentle pedaling at relaxing touring speeds. Add idyllic scenery and the end result is an exceptional mountain-bike ride. And all of this within a water-bottle's throw from downtown Boone. Who could ask for anything more?

The ride begins on a wide dirt-and-gravel road that is in good condition. There are a few potholes and rocky hills to negotiate, but for the most part, the ride poses little technical challenge. In the first mile or so, bikers can enjoy picturesque views of nearby mountains and cattle grazing the sloping green hills and valleys. Some sections of the road are crowded with the dense hardwood forests, while others are flanked by open, grassy fields. Split-rail fences, cornfields, and modest farmhouses nudge cyclists with gentle reminders of rustic civilization.

0.0 The ride begins with a left turn on Junaluska Road, now a dirt-and-gravel road.

Grinding up the hills of Junaluska Road

0.8 Firetower Road is on the left.

0.9 Indian Springs Road is on the left.

2.2 You will reach an intersection of roads at Trivett Gap. On the right is the turnoff for Howard's Knob Loop. A field is on the right and a private home is on the left. The road sign on the left says "Almost Heaven." Continue straight.

2.7 You will come to a Y-intersection; bear right to continue. On the left is Woodland Spring Lane.

5.3 You will come to the intersection of Junaluska Road and Curly Maple Road; bear left on Junaluska Road to continue.

6.2 The gravel road ends here; pavement begins. Tater Hill Road goes to the left. Bear straight onto Howard's Creek Road (S.R. 1306).

Idyllic scenery on Howard's Creek Road

7.1 Bear right on Howard's Creek Road (S.R. 1306). Sugarloaf Road bears left.

7.5 Leave the paved Howard's Creek Road by turning right onto Curly Maple Road, which is a gravel road.

8.7 Turn left onto Junaluska Road. Begin retracing your path to the starting point.

11.8 On the left is the turnoff for Howard's Knob Loop; continue straight.

13.1 Indian Springs Road is on the right.

14.0 At the stop sign, you will reach the starting point and the end of the ride.

Note: To increase the length of this ride to 17 miles, and to increase its difficulty rating to strenuous, you can begin cycling from the intersection of U.S. 321 and U.S. 421 in Boone. Follow the access directions, which will take you through a residential section of Boone. You will grind up a hill that gains 750 feet in 1.4 exhausting miles. But there is a prize for all the blood, sweat, and tears shed on the climb; the descent waiting for you at the end of the ride.

If you want an easy 3.4-mile ride, begin the ride at the intersection of Junaluska Road and Curly Maple Road (S.R. 1323) and follow the directions above until you return to this intersection.

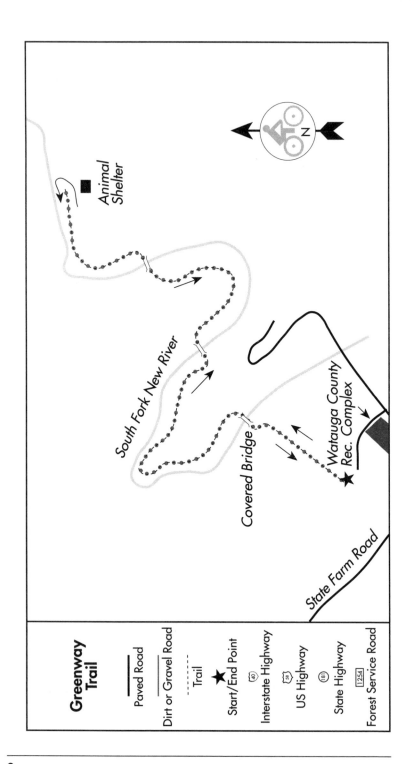

Greenway Trail

Paved Road
Dirt or Gravel Road
Trail
★ Start/End Point
Interstate Highway
US Highway
State Highway
Forest Service Road

Animal Shelter

South Fork New River

Covered Bridge

Watauga County Rec. Complex

State Farm Road

N

Boone's Greenway Trail

Distance: 6 miles

Difficulty: Easy

Riding surface: Gravel trail, dirt trail, dirt road

Map: Greenway Trail Map and Guide, available from Watauga County Parks and Recreation Department, 704 Complex Drive, Boone, N.C. 28607 (704-264-9511)

Access: From the intersection of U.S. 321 and U.S. 221 in Boone, drive south on U.S. 221 for 0.5 mile. Turn left onto State Farm Road. After about 1 mile, turn left into the Watauga County Recreation Complex. A large, paved parking area is located between the swimming pools and tennis courts.

Elevation change: There is no appreciable change in elevation.

Configuration: Out-and-back

This easy mountain-bike ride offers an ideal afternoon of two-wheeled recreation for families and beginners. The trail's surface consists of packed gravel and hard-packed dirt for its entire length. It is gently graded, with essentially no climbs. Though this trail seems custom-made for beginners and occasional cyclists, experienced cyclists enjoy it as well, due to its in-town location and natural beauty. One section of the trail is especially scenic as it winds through an area dense with mature rhododendron and majestic oak trees.

For much of its length, the trail parallels the dark waters of the South Fork of the New River, which flow like molasses down the mountain. This river is considered the oldest in America, though its name would lead you to believe otherwise. It also holds the distinction of being one of the few rivers east of the Mississippi to flow northward.

With its slowly flowing waters and occasional riffles, the New River is ideal for canoe camping. Its popularity with paddlers was boosted in the mid-1970s, when a 26-mile section was designated a National Wild and Scenic River. In 1976, President Gerald Ford found a few minutes—when he wasn't busy tripping over golf balls or falling down steps—to sign the bill. And to his credit, the National Wild and Scenic River designation forever saved the New River from being dammed.

The trail crosses the river several times on wooden bridges, the first of which is a newly constructed covered bridge. Though quaint by design, this covered bridge has not yet attained the weathered finish sported by bridges in romantic locales, such as Robert James Waller's Madison County.

When you reach the end of the trail near the animal shelter, a left turn will lead you across the river and onto Charlie Holler Road (S.R. 1515). An old cemetery located on this road may be of special interest to riders with a historical bent. Old, weather-beaten tombstones lean tiredly on a sloping, grass-covered hill. Most of the inscriptions on the stone grave markers have been muted by the forces of nature over the last 200 years, though a few are still legible. One tombstone marks the burial site of a Revolutionary War soldier.

Near the edge of the road is a rock marker informing visitors that this is also the site of the original Three Forks Baptist Church, which stood on this land in the late 1700s.

The town of Boone has extensive long-range plans to expand the length of this greenway during the next few years. You might want to check with the parks and recreation department to see if any new sections have opened. At the time of this second edition, there was one additional section that had opened. It is not included in this book because it was only a 0.4-mile loop.

0.0 Begin cycling at the far end of the parking lot. The trail skirts the edge of the tennis courts before leaving the complex.

0.4 You will cross the South Fork of the New River on a wooden covered bridge.

1.3 You will reach the New River dam site; continue cycling the trail.

1.9 A cable strung across the trail marks the end of Greenway Trail. The animal shelter is across the road on the right; if you need to refill your water bottles, you can do so at the water fountain at the animal shelter. Turn left onto the gravel road. You will immediately cross the New River over a low-water bridge and then cycle up a short hill.

2.0 At the stop sign, turn right onto Charlie Holler Road and cycle toward the cemetery, which will be on your left.

3.0 Charlie Holler Road ends at U.S. 421. Turn around and retrace your path.

6.0 You will arrive back at the starting point.

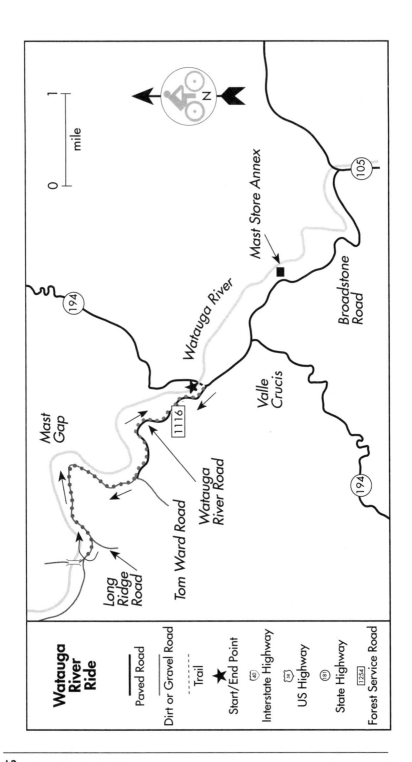

Watauga River Ride

Paved Road

Dirt or Gravel Road

Trail

★ Start/End Point

🛡40 Interstate Highway

🛡58 US Highway

🛡81 State Highway

1254 Forest Service Road

Mast Gap

Long Ridge Road

Tom Ward Road

Watauga River Road

1116

Valle Crucis

Watauga River

Mast Store Annex

Broadstone Road

194

105

194

N

mile

0   1

Watauga River Road Ride

Distance: 8 miles

Difficulty: Easy

Riding surface: Dirt road

Maps: 1. Boone/Watauga County Map
2. USGS 7.5 minute quadrangle, Valle Crucis, N.C.

Access: From U.S. 321 in downtown Boone, turn onto N.C. 105 South, heading toward Linville and Banner Elk. After 4.7 miles, turn right onto Broadstone Road at the blinking light and the sign for Valle Crucis. Drive 2.7 miles to the intersection with N.C. 194; Valle Crucis Elementary School will be on your right. Continue straight past this intersection. You will drive past the original Mast General Store, on the right. The turnoff to Watauga River Road is about a quarter-mile past the Mast General Store. If you cross the Watauga River, you have gone too far. Park at the pull-off on the right at the beginning of this road.

Elevation change: The ride begins at an elevation of 2,600 feet. It reaches a maximum of 2,750 feet near the turnaround point. The total elevation gain is 150 feet, just perfect for a leisurely Sunday-afternoon bicycle tour.

Configuration: Out-and-back

Tobacco curing in a Valle Crucis barn

asy mountain-bike rides are rather scarce in the mountain country of western North Carolina, but a gem of a ride runs along the bank of the Watauga River near the community of Valle Crucis. When this ride was selected for the first edition of this book, the cyclist rode the entire route on a hard-packed dirt road. Due to the state of North Carolina's extensive plans to pave all secondary roads, part of this route has now been paved. Because this ride is still especially good for beginning and occasional cyclists and features some of the best scenery in the area, the decision was made to keep it in this edition.

This non-technical ride offers cyclists just a bit of climbing. Not only does it offer a pleasant hour or two of pedaling, but it also winds through scenic pastureland. Early in the ride, slender hardwood trunks rise from either side of the road and create a natural tent over the road. Farther along, massive shoals of dark rock line the river; the rough texture of this rock abutting the smooth, indigo surface of the river creates a spectacular backdrop to the ride. Though the road tends to hug the bank of the Watauga River, there are several sections that curve away to thread through open fields. Attractive homes and cabins, some adorned with split-rail fences and landscaped rhododendron hedges, punctuate the natural beauty of the ride with a dose of upscale Valle Crucis civilization.

Two creeks flowing from opposite directions into Dutch Creek Valley form the shape of a cross and give the community its name, which means "Valley of the Cross." The valley, nestled in the lap of the mountains near Boone and Banner Elk, is quiet and remarkably beautiful. Regardless of whether you time your ride for sunset or earlier in the day, you are sure to find this gently rolling route quite picturesque.

The beauty of the ride is certainly enhanced by the pastoral countryside, but the Watauga River is the star of the show. The Watauga is well known by paddlers for its challenging whitewater rapids, though this placid stretch is no indication of the white-knuckle thrills boaters seek. This peaceful portion of the Watauga is known as Section II and is considered the calm before the storm.

This appetizer of a mountain-bike ride will whet your appetite for the highlights found in the Valle Crucis area. While here, you might want to take in some of the many historical sights. For starters, the original Mast General Store, built in 1883, is located within a stone's throw of the starting point of the ride. This old mercantile store, still very much in operation, stands in Valle Crucis as a prime example of turn-of-the-century Americana. Not surprisingly, there are quite a few historic bed-and-breakfast inns in the area, including the nationally renowned Mast Farm Inn and the Inn at Taylor House. For more information on the history and highlights of the Valle Crucis area, you might want to pick up a copy of *Valle Crucis* by David Yates and William Bake.

There is one special consideration to take into account before embarking on this ride. You will notice that some parts of the road are not much higher than the river at normal water

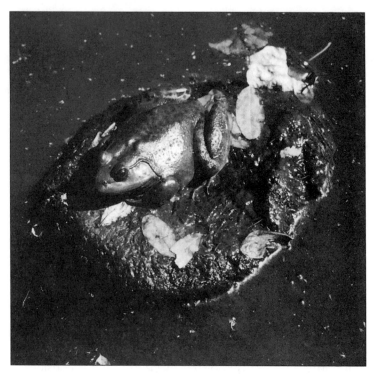
Slimy fauna found on the Watauga River

levels. With any appreciable rainfall, the swollen river quickly floods the road. If you insist on cycling this dirt road during or after inclement weather, be prepared that outriggers might be needed to keep your mountain bike from capsizing.

0.0   Begin the ride by turning left onto Watauga River Road, a paved road.

0.5   Dramatic rock outcroppings are to the left. Continue straight.

1.8   Tom Ward Road is on the left; continue straight. The pavement ends at the one-lane bridge just past Tom Ward Road.

3.8 Long Ridge Road is on the left; continue straight. During one trip along this route, the road sign was down at this location.

4.0 On the right, a bridge (this is Rominger Road) crosses the Watauga River at this point. Turn around at this point and begin retracing your path.

8.0 You will return to the stop sign at Broadstone Road, which marks the end of the ride.

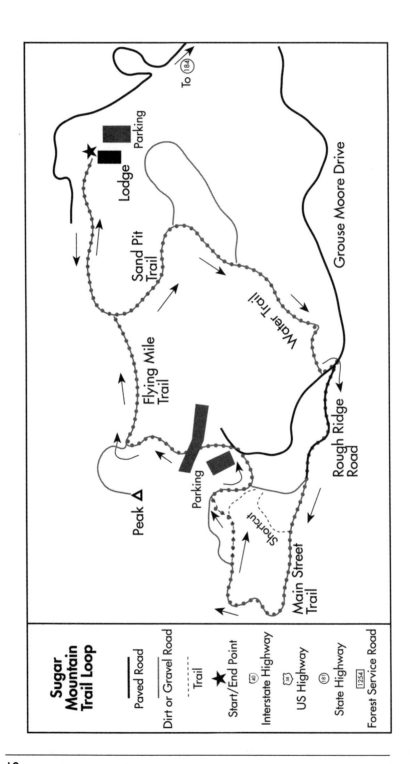

Sugar Mountain Trail Loop

Paved Road
Dirt or Gravel Road
Trail
★ Start/End Point
Interstate Highway
US Highway
State Highway
Forest Service Road

Lodge
Parking
Sand Pit Trail
Flying Mile Trail
Water Trail
Grouse Moore Drive
Peak △
Parking
Shortcut
Rough Ridge Road
Main Street Trail
To 184

Sugar Mountain Trail Loop

Distance: 5.9 miles

Difficulty: Moderate

Riding surface: Double-track trails, single-track trails, brief sections of paved roads

Map: Mountain Bike Trail Map, available from Sugar Mountain Resort, Inc., P.O. Box 369, Banner Elk N.C. 28604 (704-898-4521) or on the Internet at http://www.skisugar.com

Access: From Linville, drive north on N.C. 105 for 3.9 miles to the intersection with N.C. 184. Turn left onto N.C. 184, heading toward Banner Elk, and drive 1.5 miles to the Sugar Mountain Resort turnoff. Turn left and drive through the main entrance. Follow the signs to the ski lodge. Park in the large parking area near the lodge.

Elevation change: The ride begins at an elevation of 4,100 feet and climbs quickly, reaching a maximum elevation of about 5,200 feet near the 4-mile mark. From that point, there is a gradual loss of elevation until you reach the ski slopes. On the slopes, the elevation quickly drops back to 4,100 feet. The total elevation gain is about 1,100 feet.

Configuration: Loop

Season: This loop is open to mountain bikers only when the ski slopes are closed. Some trails not located on the ski slopes can be ridden year-round; check with the resort for current information.

*We lost count of the number of overlooks
and great views we found on this mountain biking loop.*

Gone are the ice and snow. What's left are grassy, green slopes dotted with pale gray rocks and summer's dandelions. The ski lifts are quiet, almost ghostlike, dangling forlornly in the stillness of shimmering heat. A lonely, weather-beaten ski glove rests against a clump of grass on the slope. A buckle and a dark blue, torn piece of a bib overall strap lie across the trail. A broken ski pole sticks out of a bush, calling up an image of a frustrated, angry skier who probably was forced to descend the icy slopes with the help of only balance and luck.

This is an off-season look at Sugar Mountain Ski Resort. Though it may paint a bleak picture for skiers, it sparks the antennae of mountain bikers, who know how good riding can be on off-season ski slopes. And Sugar Mountain hasn't let cyclists down; the resort boasts over 20 miles of single- and double-track trails. A free brochure from the resort has a map of the trails, but be sure to ask someone at the desk which trails are open to bikers. You can also ask about events that the resort hosts for bikers during summer months.

Though it stops just short of bumping your bike computer up to a reading of 6 miles, this short ride is tough. Sugar

Mountain's special-events coordinator, Kim Schmidinger, describes it as "really pretty strenuous."

While the ride is certainly challenging, it may not be as torturous as you are expecting. Beginning on a rocky double-track trail, it wastes no time in making you drop into your small chain ring. You may find your typical early-ride whatcha-been-up-to-lately conversations coming to a quick halt. The climbing ends at the top of the ski slope, as does the open scenery. The next leg of the loop is a narrow, rolling single-track trail tucked into a dense forest. You won't see the ski slopes again until the end of the ride.

Well marked and easy to follow, this loop offers a combination of climbs and fun, moderately technical descents. Occasional overlooks near the trails give mountain bikers panoramic vistas of nearby mountains, including those of neighboring ski resorts. Much of the ride is shady and cool, while other portions will pop you into open areas where the sun will glaze your shoulders.

Near the end of the ride, you'll have a chance to blast through a beautiful green glade shaded by occasional tall hardwood trees. Thrilling to pedal, this narrow, single-track section of trail weaves around tree trunks and visits pockets of dense foliage hiding rocks and tricky trail obstructions. In the spring, a luxuriant carpet of feathery ground cover will tickle your ankles if you drift from the center of the trail. Popping up through all this greenness are purple trillium, violets, and little daisies. Huge yellow buckeye trees tower overhead and help block out the heat. This sweet stretch of trail doesn't last long, unfortunately. You will soon be spinning along the grassy double track again.

Finally, the trail descends until it deposits you at the top of the ski slope you rode up earlier. Now it's time to go back down. No snowplowing this time of year—this is the season for fat tires. If a straight shot down the slope is a little too vertical for your taste, then do as the skiers do and traverse the slope from side to side. You can control your speed better, and the downhill grade won't be nearly so formidable.

Note: Sugar Mountain Resort is the first ski resort in the

Boone/Banner Elk area to develop mountain-biking trails as part of its efforts to attract vacationers year-round. The resort doesn't charge a fee to ride the trails, but it does require that cyclists wear helmets.

0.0   Begin riding at the base of Sugar Mountain Resort, at the bottom of Easy Street Slope (the brown lift). Locate the green trail markers and begin following them up the edge of the slope on a rocky double-track trail to the left of the chair lift. You will begin climbing immediately.

0.3   Bear left, following the trail markers.

0.4   You will pass under the ski lift and come to the top of a hill; there is a nice view to the left. Turn right here. A green trail marker with an arrow shows the direction of the loop.

0.5   Turn left at the next green trail marker. You will cycle up a bank, go through an opening in the wooden fence, and then turn left at the fence. You will pedal around the red "bull wheel"—or turnaround station—of the ski lift and then begin another climb.

0.6   At the green ski lift, there is a view of Hawksnest Ski Resort to the left. You will continue straight and start descending a wide, tree-lined double-track trail. This is called Sand Pit Trail.

0.8   The Sky Leaf condominiums are on the right. The trail you are pedaling is actually an easement that allows skiers direct access to the slopes during winter.

0.9   You will pedal into a sandy clearing. Continue following the green trail markers, heading straight on a rocky double track.

Some parts of Sugar Mountain Trail Loop pass right under the ski lift.

1.3 You will come to an intersection with a trail designated by yellow markers. Turn right and begin following the yellow trail makers. (If you go straight, you will come to a pump house.) You can hear a stream trickling through the woods. After this turn, you will begin climbing on a double-track trail with a moderately technical surface of gravel and dirt. This is called Water Trail. You will pass several pump houses along the way.

1.7 The trail ends at Grouse Moore Drive, a paved road. On the left are the Misty Woods condominiums. Pass through the brown metal gate at the condominiums. Continue following the yellow trail markers by turning left onto Grouse Moore Road, then immediately right onto Rough Ridge Road. You will descend on this rough-textured paved road.

2.2 The pavement ends. Continue straight on a double-track trail with a gravel and dirt surface. This is Main Street

Trail. Continue following the yellow trail markers. At this point, you can see Linville Ridge on the left. Horse stables are located on fenced private property on the left. On the right is a trail with orange markers, a difficult technical climb.

2.5 Bear left at the fork, staying on the rocky double-track trail.

3.4 Turn right onto the single-track trail known as Sherwood Avenue. There is a yellow sign with a blue arrow at this turn.

3.6 Turn left at the fork in the trail. You will emerge onto a grassy double-track trail again.

3.7 Turn right onto the single-track Williams Trail.

3.9 Turn right onto the grassy double-track Main Street Trail.

4.3 Turn left at the intersection with the paved Grouse Moore Drive. Sugar Top condominiums are on the left.

4.5 Turn left at the stop sign and follow the yellow trail markers through the parking lot of the condominium complex.

4.6 Turn right at the sign designating buildings numbered 2, 3, and 4.

4.7 Turn left at building #3. When you turn left at building #3, you will be at the bottom of the parking lot. Go around a green metal gate and begin pedaling across the ski slopes on the double-track Cat Trace Trail. On the right is a good view of Hanging Rock and the surrounding mountains. You will pass under the green chair lift, heading toward the yellow chair lift.

4.8 Pass under the yellow chair lift. There is a great view on the right. Your main objective now is to reach the lodge at the bottom of the Easy Street ski slope. You can follow the path under the yellow chair lift or cut back and forth across slopes under the red and yellow lifts using the short single-track trails which cut through the narrow patches of trees separating the two slopes.

There is also the option of riding Lizard Lane, an extremely technical trail that cuts off from the slope under the yellow lift. This trail is part of the course that is used for the "Showdown at Sugar" bike race held in October. It is for experienced riders only.

5.9 You will return to the starting point at the main lodge building.

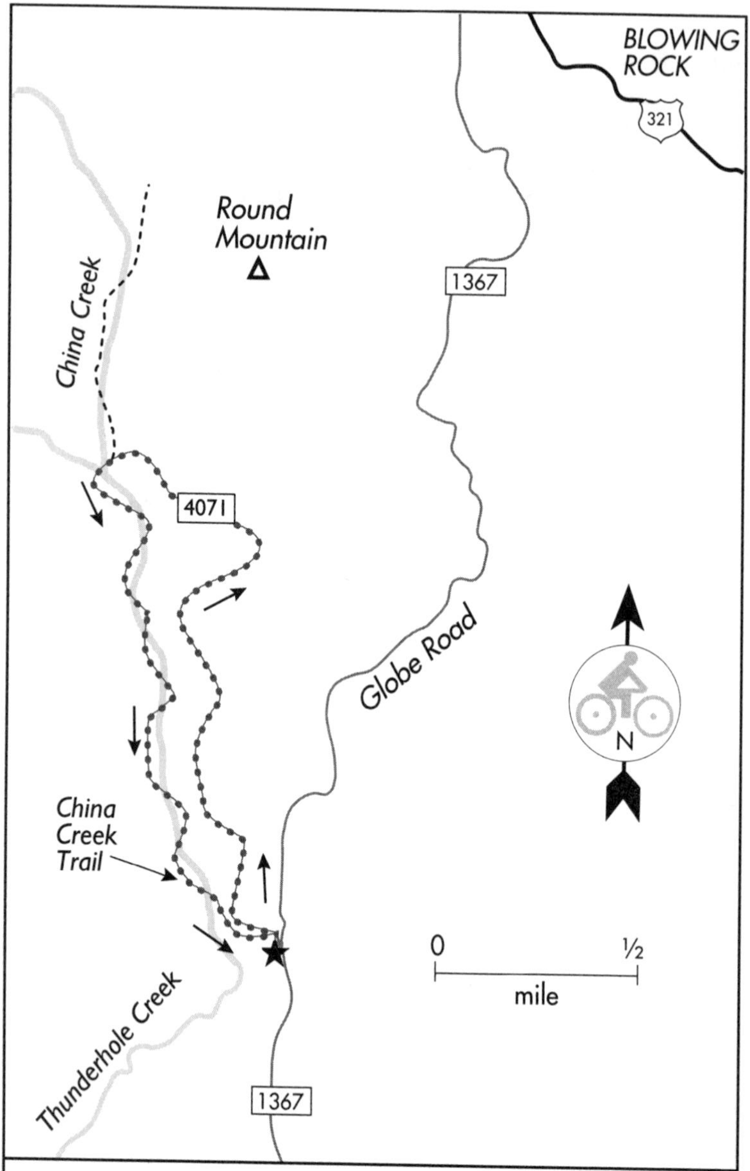
BLOWING ROCK
321
Round Mountain
China Creek
1367
4071
Globe Road
N
China Creek Trail
0
½
mile
Thunderhole Creek
1367

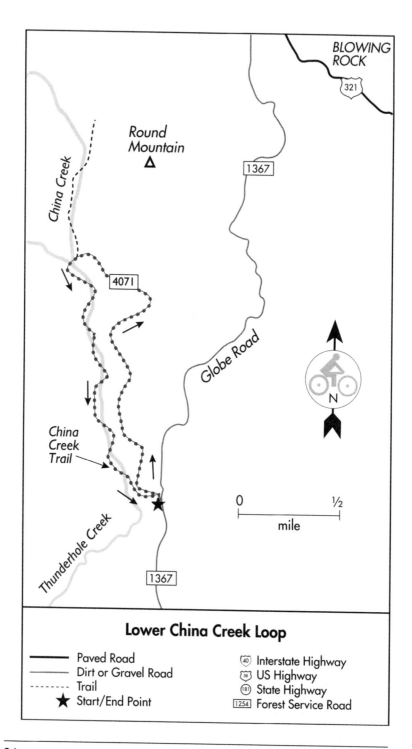

Lower China Creek Loop

Paved Road
Dirt or Gravel Road
Trail
Start/End Point
40 Interstate Highway
58 US Highway
181 State Highway
1254 Forest Service Road

Lower China Creek Loop

Distance: 4.4 miles

Difficulty: Moderate

Riding Surface: Dirt road, single-track trail

Maps: 1. Pisgah National Forest: Grandfather District
2. USGS 7.5 minute quadrangle, Globe, N.C.
3. Pisgah National Forest: Wilson Creek Area Trail Map
4. Outdoor Recreation Map and Guide, Boone, N.C., region, from Blue Planet Publishing, Inc., P.O. Box 9195, Boone, N.C. 28608

Access: From the junction of U.S. 321 and U.S. 221 in Blowing Rock, drive south on U.S. 321 Business (or Main Street) for 0.4 mile. At the second street past the Rumple Memorial Presbyterian Church, turn right onto Johns River Road (S.R. 1367). There is a sign here that reads "Globe 8." Drive approximately 3.2 miles to a pull-off on the right. This pull-off is not marked, so watch your mileage. It is next to F.R. 4071, which is unmarked. Approximately 30 yards from the road, you will see signs identifying the boundary for North Carolina wildlife gamelands. Park at the pull-off.

Elevation change: The ride begins at an elevation of about 1,750 feet and climbs steadily along the dirt road to a maximum of about 2,000 feet at the intersection with China Creek Trail. It then drops back to 1,750 feet on its return to the starting point. The total elevation gain is 250 feet.

Configuration: Loop

Try doing this with a skinny-tired racing bike!

Short and sweet, this mountain-bike loop offers an ideal ride for cyclists just looking for an hour's spin in the woods. Although it is short and has little elevation change, there are rocky and technical sections. It is so close to Blowing Rock that you can almost see the trailhead from Main Street. The ride can be lengthened and the difficulty increased by pedaling straight from town and humming down Globe Road to the turnoff. You will have a grind of a climb back into town, though, gaining 1,750 feet of elevation in only 3.5 miles.

Half the loop is on a forest-service road that curls up toward the junction of China Creek and Thunderhole Creek. The other half is on a beautiful stretch of descending single track that flirts with the banks of Thunderhole Creek. There are six frigid creek crossings that will take your breath away if you fail to negotiate them successfully. Mountain bikers have given the creek's name new meaning, their cries thundering through the forest after an icy spill. Make sure you check for high-water possibilities before attempting this ride.

Creatures on two wheels aren't the only varmints you're likely to run into on this trail. You might see a cobalt blue salamander sunning itself on a smooth, gray river rock, or a friendly garter snake working on its tan. Cock an ear to the forest and you might hear a squirrel foraging for nuts or birds at play. The dense woods are filled with white-tailed deer, wild turkey, and grouse.

The minimal elevation gain, easy access, tolerable length, and pleasant surroundings make this an ideal ride for beginning mountain-bikers to try their luck at single-track riding.

0.0 You will begin pedaling a dirt road that starts with a gradual climb. You will see the North Carolina wildlife gamelands sign near the entrance to this road.

1.4 You will pedal across New Year's Creek on a concrete bridge.

1.9 Bear left on a dirt road. A jeep road intersects from the right.

2.4 Cross through Thunderhole Creek on a concrete pad. Straight ahead there are two dirt tank traps. Pass over

Don't scream—it's just a friendly little garter snake catching some rays.

these tank traps and turn left onto the single-track China Creek Trail. Do not take the old logging road that is straight ahead of the tank traps.

2.8 Cross Thunderhole Creek again.

3.1 Cross Thunderhole Creek a third time.

3.3 Bear right, and cross the creek a fourth time.

3.5 Cross the creek a fifth time.

3.7 Cross the creek for the sixth time.

3.9 You will ascend for 0.1 mile on a steep rocky stretch to F.R. 4071.

4.0 Turn right onto the dirt F.R. 4071.

4.4 Arrive back at the pull-off where you parked.

Northwest North Carolina
<u>Pisgah National Forest:Wilson Creek Area</u>

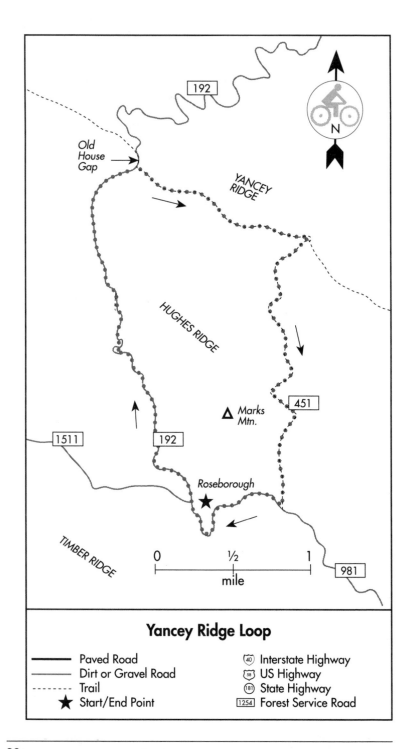

Yancey Ridge Loop

▬▬▬ Paved Road	⑩ Interstate Highway
▬▬▬ Dirt or Gravel Road	⑱ US Highway
- - - - Trail	⑱ State Highway
★ Start/End Point	1254 Forest Service Road

Yancey Ridge Loop

Distance: 8.1 miles

Difficulty: Moderate to strenuous

Riding surface: Dirt road, four-wheel-drive road

Maps: 1. Wilson Creek Area Trail Map
2. USGS 7.5 minute quadrangle, Grandfather Mountain, N.C.
3. Outdoor Recreation Map and Guide, Boone, N.C., region, from Blue Planet Publishing, Inc., P.O. Box 9195, Boone, N.C. 28608

Access: From the intersection of U.S. 221 and N.C. 105 in Linville, drive south on U.S. 221. After approximately 0.2 mile, turn left onto Roseborough Road (S.R. 1511) at the four-way stop; this is the second left after the intersection of U.S. 221 and N.C. 105. Roseborough Road is paved for 1.6 miles until it changes to dirt when it reaches the Blue Ridge Parkway. As you continue on Roseborough Road, you will be descending through scenic surroundings. Rattlesnake Cliffs loom over the road at the 3-mile mark. Some 6.7 miles from the traffic light in Linville, you will arrive at a pull-over. You can park here or cross the bridge to park at another parking area on the right.

Elevation change: This loop begins at an elevation of 2,000 feet. It steadily climbs to 3,000 feet over the next 3 miles until you reach the turnoff at Old House Gap. You then climb 100 feet before the trail levels off and begins to descend. By the turnoff to Marks Mountain, the elevation drops to 2,600 feet. The road continues on a gently descending grade, reaching 2,400 feet at F.R. 981. This dirt road will return you to the starting point and an elevation of 2,000 feet. The total elevation gain is 1,100 feet.

Configuration: Loop

The Wilson Creek area has long been regarded by local mountain bikers as a haven for off-road cycling. Though only two single-track trails are currently designated for mountain-bike use, there are myriad other ride possibilities in this area. Miles and miles of gated forest-service roads wind through these beautiful, green mountains. Fortunately, mountain bikers are welcome to pedal all of these dirt roads. Though many such narrow dirt tracks are classified as roads, most cyclists would be hard-pressed to describe them as anything other than *trails*.

Yancey Ridge Loop, probably the most popular of all Wilson Creek's mountain-bike rides, is a perfect example. This moderately strenuous loop consists of old logging roads and four-wheel-drive roads, though you would swear that you're on single-track trails for much of the ride.

The ride begins on F.R. 192, a gently climbing dirt-and-gravel road flanked by towering hardwood trees. The woods are punctuated by stately hemlock trees rising from an understory of dark green rhododendron. After a mile or so of steady climbing, the grade steepens to a strenuous grind up the west side of Hughes Ridge. If you have not worked up a sweat by the time you reach the turnoff at Old House Gap, then you must be dead.

The climb continues for a short distance on a rough four-wheel-drive road on top of Yancey Ridge, but it soon subsides. This old logging road has suffered from erosion; the ditches left behind will thrill hammerhead cyclists. Hard-core mountain bikers will love this technically challenging section. Others may want to simply dismount and push their bikes, offering all kinds of pitiful excuses—down to a sore throat—for not riding this extremely technical section.

If you manage to lift your eyes from the rocky, technical trail unrolling before your wheels, there are occasional spots along the ridge top that offer glimpses of the nearby mountains. These beautiful views all but disappear during summer, when the hard-woods are at their verdant, leafy finest.

The ride continues with a right turn onto F.R. 451, which drops down the east side of Marks Mountain. This turn is easy to miss, so watch carefully as you near the bottom of the hill. This is a fast leg offering some logs to jump or bunny-hop and some technical sections to negotiate. A final right turn onto F.R. 981 brings the loop to a close.

0.0   If you parked in the pull-over area before the concrete bridge, cross the bridge and turn left onto F.R. 192, the first dirt road on the left. If you parked in the parking area across from F.R. 192, pedal across the road and start the climb up this dirt-and-gravel road.

2.1   There is a good view of the creek below you to the left. Look for cascades.

Cyclists making the turn off Yancey Ridge

Rocky sections on Yancey Ridge call for some technical riding.

2.2 Bear right

2.7 Bear right. There is a gated road on the left.

3.0 You have reached Old House Gap. There is a double yellow blaze on a pine tree at this intersection. Turn right onto Yancey Ridge Trail. Look for the marker that reads 451 and climb 0.1 mile on this trail.

3.2 Bear left, crest the hill, and descend.

4.1 There is a clearing with a spring on the left.

4.4 Turn right at a sharp turn at the base of the hill. You are now descending on F.R. 451. This is a confusing intersection, as there are three unmarked trails here. Take the route that descends to your fartherest right.

5.7 As the road levels out, there is a nice view of the grassy forest on the left.

6.0 Start a short climb.

6.7 The road levels.

7.1 Turn right onto F.R. 981, a wide, well-groomed dirt road.

8.1 You will arrive back at the starting point.

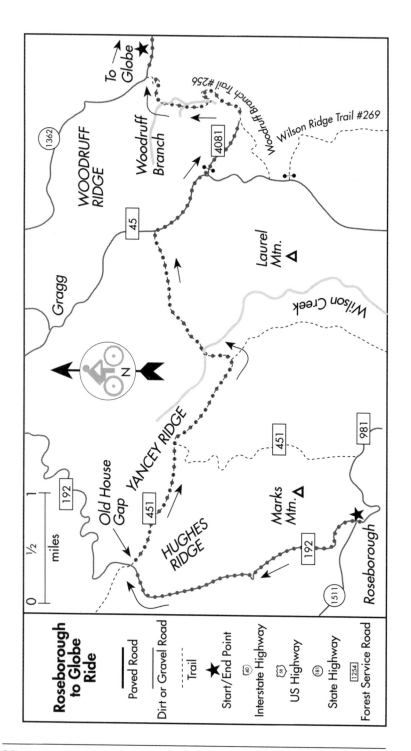

Roseborough to Globe Ride

- Paved Road
- Dirt or Gravel Road
- Trail
- ★ Start/End Point
- 40 Interstate Highway
- 58 US Highway
- 81 State Highway
- 1254 Forest Service Road

To Globe ★

WOODRUFF RIDGE

(1362)

Gragg

Woodruff Branch

Woodruff Branch Trail #256

4081

45

Wilson Ridge Trail #269

Laurel Mtn. △

Wilson Creek

N

YANCEY RIDGE

Old House Gap

192

451

451

981

1

½

0

miles

HUGHES RIDGE

Marks Mtn. △

192

1511

Roseborough ★

Roseborough to Globe Ride

Distance: 12.4 miles

Difficulty: Moderate to strenuous

Riding surface: Dirt road, single-track trail, paved road

Maps: 1. Wilson Creek Area Trail Map
2. Pisgah National Forest: Grandfather District
3. USGS 7.5 minute quadrangle, Grandfather Mountain, N.C.
4. USGS 7.5 minute quadrangle, Globe, N.C.
5. Outdoor Recreation Map and Guide, Boone, N.C., region, from Blue Planet Publishing, Inc., P.O. Box 9195, Boone, N.C. 28608

Access: To reach the Roseborough access, drive south on U.S. 221 from the intersection of U.S. 221 and N.C. 105 in Linville. After approximately 0.2 mile, turn left onto Roseborough Road (S.R. 1511) at the four-way stop; this is the second left after the intersection of U.S. 221 and N.C. 105. Roseborough Road is paved for 1.6 miles until it changes to dirt when it reaches the Blue Ridge Parkway. As you continue on Roseborough Road, you will be descending through scenic surroundings. Rattlesnake Cliffs loom over the road at the 3-mile mark. Some 6.7 miles from the traffic light in Linville, you will arrive at a pullover. You can park here or cross the bridge to park at another parking area on the right.

To reach the Globe access, drive south from the junction of U.S. 321 and U.S. 221 in Blowing Rock on U.S. 321 Business (or Main Street) for 0.4 mile. At the second street past the Rumple Memorial Presbyterian Church, turn right onto Johns River Road (S.R. 1367). There is a sign here that reads "Globe 8." Drive approximately 8 miles to the end of the road. Globe Baptist Church is straight ahead. Turn right and park at the pull-off on the right next to the creek.

Elevation change: This ride begins at an elevation of 2,000 feet in Roseborough. It steadily climbs, reaching 3,000 feet at the turnoff at Old House Gap. After a short ascent at the start of Yancey Ridge Trail, the ride levels off and begins descending, though there are still a few hills thrown in to keep you honest. The elevation drops to 2,000 feet at Wilson Creek. A climb follows on an old logging road which takes you to F.R. 45 and an elevation of 2,500 feet. At the gated turnoff to Woodruff Branch Trail, the elevation is 2,600 feet and the climbing is over. You will drop to 1,350 feet by the time you reach your shuttle vehicle in Globe. The total elevation gain is about 1,600 feet.

Configuration: One-way

Safety note: Check the water level in the area creeks before attempting this ride. If the water level is high, crossing Wilson Creek can be dangerous.

This is one of the classic mountain-bike rides in the high country of western North Carolina. Though "classic mountain-bike ride" tends to conjure up images of places like Moab and Tsali, where there are hordes of cyclists and wall-to-wall Lycra and titanium, this ride doesn't fall into that category. Though local cyclists often pedal this route, you may find yourself alone on these trails. Solitude seekers, you had better enjoy it while you can. There's no way a gem of a ride like this will remain in the shadows.

You will start pedaling on F.R. 192 right in the teeth of a pretty tough climb. You will gain 1,000 feet of elevation by the time you pedal into Old House Gap, only 3 miles from the starting point in Roseborough. Make friends with your small chain ring, because you will be intimate with it for several long stretches on this ride.

You will then turn onto F.R. 451, a moderately technical four-wheel-drive track. You will do some climbing, but it is the descents you will remember later. You can plunge straight down the great downhills on this stretch for a thrilling ride. Or you can weave from side to side, carving brisk turns on the basin-shaped banks of the road.

As good as this four-wheel-drive path is for mountain biking, just wait until you zip down the technical single track that spills into Wilson Creek. The trail might not be the only thing spilling into the creek, because the rocks are slippery. The opposite side of the creek is a jumble of large boulders, perfect for propping up your soggy feet to dry them out. What follows is a tough, technical climb that seems to last forever. A stretch of exquisite single track waits, so hunker down, pedal on, and get this climb over with.

Woodruff Branch Trail is a single-track treasure. Fallen pine

Remnants of an old chimney stand near the trail.

needles blanket the trail and muffle the sound of spinning tires. The smell of flowering trees such as Fraser magnolias occasionally wafts over you as you pedal. White pines crowd the trail and reach out to tickle and prick your bare arms as you blast through the woods.

If you think it just can't get any better than this, think again. You are about to pedal down to a rushing waterfall tucked away in a pocket of pristine wilderness. A tranquil pool shimmers at the base of the fall and might just lure you in for a dip on a hot summer day.

The final leg of this exceptional ride is along Anthony Creek Road, a dirt road that changes to pavement. Rolling countryside fans out on either side of the road, and shrubbery farms, tree farms, and nurseries dot the landscape. There are no climbs and no descents on this road. It is just a peaceful stretch of pavement that offers a perfect ending to one of the best mountain-bike rides in northwest North Carolina.

0.0   If you parked in the pull-over area before the concrete bridge, cross the bridge and turn left onto F.R. 192, the first dirt road on the left. If you parked in the parking area across from F.R. 192, pedal across the road and start the climb up this dirt-and-gravel road.

2.1   There is a good view of the creek below you to the left. Look for cascades.

2.2   Bear right

2.7   Bear right. There is a gated road on the left.

3.0   You have reached Old House Gap. There is a double yellow blaze on a pine tree at this intersection. Turn right onto Yancey Ridge Trail. Look for the marker that reads 451 and climb 0.1 mile on this trail.

3.2   Bear left, crest the hill, and descend.

3.6   Bear right to continue on the main trail. There is a gated road on the left.

4.1   There is a clearing on the left. A spring is located here.

4.3   Continue straight on Yancey Ridge Trail. F.R. 451 turns off to the right at this intersection. The trails at this intersection are not marked, so be alert.

5.4   You will see a faded orange blaze on a tree to your left. Turn left onto a single-track trail. You will immediately start a technical descent.

5.8   You will cross Wilson Creek. This creek crossing is a walker. After crossing, turn left and push your bike through some boulders to find the trail again. You will cross two small tributaries of Wilson Creek before proceeding up another short, steep bank.

6.0   After pushing up a rocky slope, you will come out onto an old logging road; a grove of pine tree and a small cabin are to the left of the road. Follow the logging road.

6.1   Cross a creek.

6.2   There is a chimney on the left. Past the chimney you will have another creek crossing. In the next 0.3 mile, you will cross the creek two more times.

6.6   You will cross the creek another time. There is a sign here that reads "Cary Flat Branch." You will now start to climb.

7.2   Go around the metal gate and continue on the road.

7.3   Turn right onto F.R. 45, a dirt road. There are small houses in this area.

8.1   At the top of the hill, turn left toward Woodruff Branch Trail #256. There is a directional marker at this spot. Go around a white metal gate and proceed down the grassy double track.

8.9   Woodruff Trail turns off to the left, where it becomes a narrow single-track trail. It is marked by a red round blaze and a directional marker reading "Woodruff Trail #256."

9.0   Cross the logging road and continue following the red round blazes of Woodruff Trail.

9.2   Cross the logging road again and continue on Woodruff Trail. The faded red blaze is on a tree to the right.

9.4   The trail ends on a technical, steep stretch spiced with water bars. Turn right onto the logging road, pedal about 50 yards, and then turn left to return to Woodruff Branch Trail. There is a directional marker on the left to mark the turn onto the trail, but it may be difficult to see.

9.5   You will begin a steep descent, followed by a ride through a patch of slick boulders. Right after the rocks, you will cross a small creek.

10.0   You will pedal across a creek. The remnants of a stone chimney are on the right.

10.2   You will cross the creek again.

10.3   The trail surface changes to rock. On the left are the headwaters of Woodruff Branch waterfall. This is a treacherous section of trail, so use caution. You can hike a short distance down to the 75-foot waterfall. At the base of the fall is an inviting pool you might want to cool off in during the summer.

10.6 You will reach the end of Woodruff Branch Trail. Turn right onto Anthony Creek Road (S.R. 1362), a dirt-and-gravel road.

11.1 The gravel road changes to pavement. On the left is Rackett Creek Place (S.R. 1361); continue straight on Anthony Creek Road.

12.4 You will arrive at Globe Baptist Church. Globe Road (S.R. 1367) turns off to the left. This is the end of the ride.

Woodruff Branch Waterfall—a pleasant highlight toward the end of the ride

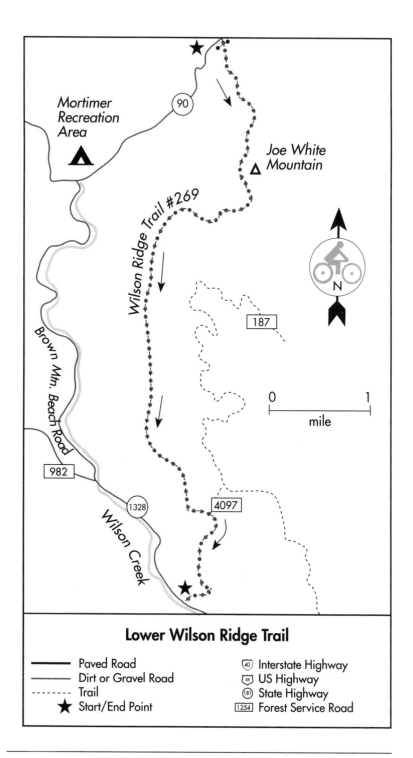

Mortimer
Recreation
Area

90

Joe White
Mountain

Wilson Ridge Trail #269

Brown Mtn. Beach Road

187

N

0   1
mile

982

1328

4097

Wilson Creek

Lower Wilson Ridge Trail

————— Paved Road
————— Dirt or Gravel Road
---------- Trail
★ Start/End Point

40 Interstate Highway
58 US Highway
181 State Highway
1254 Forest Service Road

Lower Wilson Ridge Trail

Distance: 8.5 miles

Difficulty: Moderate to strenuous

Riding surface: Single-track trail, old logging road, dirt road

Maps: 1. Wilson Creek Area Trail Map
        2. Pisgah National Forest: Grandfather District
        3. USGS 7.5 minute quadrangle, Collettsville, N.C.

Access: To reach the S.R. 90 access, drive south approximately 0.2 mile on U.S. 221 from the intersection of U.S. 221 and N.C. 105 in Linville. Turn left onto Roseborough Road (S.R. 1511) at the four-way stop; this is the second left after the intersection of U.S. 221 and N.C. 105. Roseborough Road is paved for 1.6 miles until it changes to dirt when it reaches the Blue Ridge Parkway. Drive 8.8 miles until you reach the T-intersection with S.R. 90. Turn right and drive 2 miles to Mortimer Recreation Area. Continue on S.R. 90 another 2.5 miles; the gated, old logging road which is the Lower Wilson Ridge trailhead is on the right. Though there is no trail signpost, a blue triangle is nailed to a tree on the right.

To reach the Brown Mountain Beach access, follow the above directions to Mortimer Recreation Area. Turn onto Brown Mountain Beach Road (S.R. 1328) and drive 4 miles to the bridge across Wilson Creek. Continue straight for another 1.9 miles to the end of Wilson Ridge Trail, which is on the left. There are some large rocks at the end of the trail, a brown "vehicle parking" sign, and a blue triangle on a tree. Leave your vehicle at any of the many pull-offs near the trail.

Elevation change: The trail begins at an elevation of 2,200 feet and climbs quickly to 2,600 feet. After a few dips, it climbs Joe White Mountain to an elevation of a little more than 2,800 feet. A descent to 2,400 feet follows before the climbing resumes. The trail reaches nearly 2,600 feet again, then makes a final drop to a minimum of 1,300 feet. The total elevation gain is 800 feet.

Configuration: One-way

Feel robust? Feel like a little two-wheeled exploration? Feel like pulling out the ol' compass and map and trying to figure out just where the heck you are? Well, maybe you won't have to do all that, but people have been known to greet nightfall while still out on Wilson Ridge Trail.

If you have a tendency to get lost, better try another ride in this guidebook. Though the High Country Mountain Bike Association worked hard several years ago to mark and clear this trail, there are still some sections that are pretty darn tricky. Rather than the trees being blazed with colored paint, blue triangles have been nailed to them to mark the route. These triangles don't exactly jump out when you are pedaling along at breakneck speed. There are also some significant turns that might be hard to notice even if they were marked with blinking neon signs. When this book was updated, there had been little recent maintenance on the trail. There were several blowdowns blocking parts of the trail and several deeply eroded gullies were impossible to ride. Trail conditions may be improved by the time you attempt this ride.

Your first time on this trail, you might consider checking with some of the Boone bike shops to see if you can join a planned ride. Or find someone who knows the trail well, and go with that person. Or try dropping breadcrumbs to find your way out, but we all know where that landed Gretel. At the very least, make sure that you or someone in your group has the topographical maps for this ride, as well as a compass. A

Taking a break after a tough climb

bike computer will also greatly help in following the directions in this chapter. Getting lost in these hills is a real possibility.

For those of you who haven't been scared way, despite the nebulous nature of this route, this is really a great mountain-bike ride. Even though it is less than 9 miles long, this trail is a true challenge. In a nutshell, this is a ride of extremes: extreme climbs, extreme downhills, and extreme beauty.

Some of the climbs are straight-up grinds, while others are stairstep ascents. Some of the downhills are simple plunges, while others are downright wild. Whipping through the forest around bends on technical, deeply rutted, nearly vertical surfaces is like paddling a kayak into the Chattooga River's infamous Bull Sluice rapid. Well, not quite. But it is thrilling, just the same. If you're looking for gentle climbs and easy downhills, then you'd better look elsewhere, for the mountains of Wilson Ridge are going to sock it to you.

On a tamer note, Wilson Ridge Trail is as aesthetically pleasing as it is heart-pounding. The trail weaves through dense forests of oak, hickory, and maple, dotted with a variety of wildflowers during the warm months. Columbine, wild iris, and fire pinks—to name just a few—are prolific along the trail. The blossoms of mountain silverbell trees and the fuzzy yellow flowers of sweetleaf trees will bathe your nose with their sweet fragrances as you pedal past.

Leaving the woods, the trail occasionally shoots into open clearings that offer expansive views of nearby mountains and valleys. At the upper end of the trail, you will see a mountain off to the right that looks like the dorsal fin of a shark. This is Table Rock Mountain, the giant stone chameleon of Pisgah National Forest. You can view this mountain from north, south, east, and west, and its appearance will be different from each vantage.

0.0 After leaving a shuttle vehicle at the end of the trail on Brown Mountain Beach Road, begin the ride on S.R. 90. Cycle around the white metal gate and proceed up the grassy, old logging road.

0.1 Bear right at the fork and continue climbing through a grove of small locust saplings.

0.2 You will come to a clear-cut section. Look carefully for a blue triangle blaze nailed to a tree on the right. Turn right and proceed up the steep bank onto the single track marked by this blaze. Behind you is a nice view of Table Rock Mountain on the right and Grandmother Mountain with its radio tower on the left.

0.3 You will enter the woods on the climbing single-track trail.

0.4 Turn right as the trail intersects an old logging road.

1.0 Turn right at a very sharp turn in the logging road. Do not take the single-track trail that goes straight ahead.

1.5 There are posted signs on either side of the trail. Stay on the trail and off this private property.

2.0 A white cabin is on the right; continue straight.

2.4 There is a cable strung across an old logging road on the right. Continue straight on a double-track logging road.

2.6 After passing a private drive with a red gate and a mail box on the left, you will bear right. Just past this drive, you will pedal around a huge mud puddle in the trail. Cables are strung between trees on either side of the trail. Just past these cables are double blue triangles nailed into a tree on the right; these indicate a change of direction. Turn left onto a narrow, rutted, climbing single-track trail. On the right after the turn, you can see a blue triangle on a small tree. If you miss this turn, you will come to a closed red gate just around the bend.

2.8 At the top of the climb, there is a beautiful view on the left.

3.8 Begin climbing a very steep, extremely rutted section of the trail that climbs straight up the hill for 0.1 mile. Again, there is a blue triangle on a tree here.

4.2 A very large tree lies across the trail. There is a path on the left that horses have made when going around this obstruction. You will also see some flagging tape in the trees here.

4.3 Bear right onto a single-track trail. You will see some flagging tape in the trees alongside this rutted trail.

4.4 Go to the left of another tree in the trail. You will see more flagging tape. Just past this tree, the trail begins another steep climb.

4.8 The trail turns off to the left and merges into an old logging road.

5.0 The trail emerges into a clear-cut area with a nice view. Continue descending on a grassy, old logging road.

6.5 Continue straight on the logging road. There is a steep bank on the right.

6.7 Bear right on the logging road. There is a road that bears left, but stay on the right-hand road.

7.0 At the T-intersection, bear right onto the smooth old logging road. There is an old, rough road on the extreme right. Avoid that route. Stay on the more-travelled road.

Picking a line on a technical stretch of single track

7.1   Bear right at the Y-intersection.

7.2   Turn left onto the single track at this gravel turnaround. On the left near the start of this trail, you will see a blue triangle blaze on a tree. You will immediately ride over 3 small dirt "whoop-te-dos." You will have to maneuver around many roots and rocks on this very technical descent.

7.6   Bear left onto the single-track trail.

8.0   At the Y-intersection, turn right onto the single track. You can hear the roar of Wilson Creek from this point on.

8.5   You will intersect with Brown Mountain Beach Road. The trail ends here.

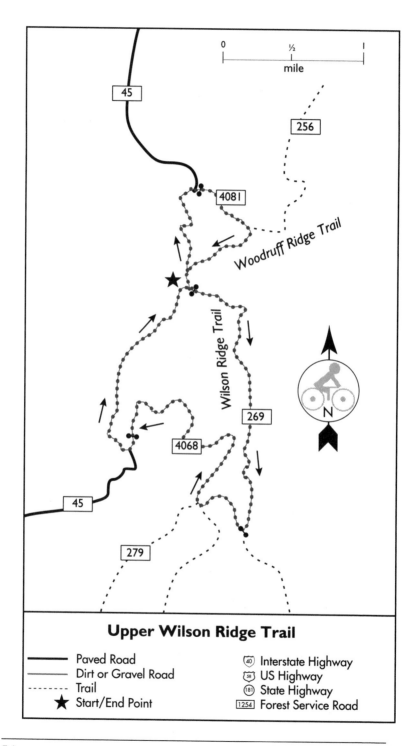

Upper Wilson Ridge Trail

—— Paved Road	ⓐ⁰	Interstate Highway
~~ Dirt or Gravel Road	⑤⁸	US Highway
----- Trail	⑱	State Highway
★ Start/End Point	1254	Forest Service Road

Upper Wilson Ridge Trail

Distance: 9.7 miles

Difficulty: Moderate

Riding Surface: Dirt-and-gravel road, single-track trail

Maps: 1. USGS 7.5 minute quadrangle, Grandfather Mountain, N.C.
2. USGS 7.5 minute quadrangle, Globe, N.C.
3. Wilson Creek Area Trail Map
4. Outdoor Recreation Map and Guide, Boone, N.C., region, from Blue Planet Publishing, Inc., P.O. Box 9195, Boone, N.C. 28608

Access: From the intersection of U.S. 221 & N.C. 105 in Linville, turn left onto U.S. 221, heading toward Grandfather Mountain. At milepoint 2.1, the entrance to Grandfather Mountain will be on the left. At milepoint 3.1, continue on U.S. 221 as it passes under the Blue Ridge Parkway. At milepoint 3.6, turn right onto S.R. 1514 (Edgemont Road), a gravel road. There are very good views of Grandfather and the other mountains in this area along this route. There is also a scenic view of Wilson Creek at one of the bridges along the road. At milepoint 8.9, you will pass through the community of Gragg. At milepoint 9.1, bear right onto S.R. 1514. Globe Road turns off to the left. The road you are on is marked F.R. 45 after you enter the national-forest area. At milepoint 10.9, bear left at the fork to continue on F.R. 45. At milepoint 12.6, there is a large parking area on the left. Park here, but do not block the gate. The metal gate that is constructed from an old guardrail is the Wilson Ridge trailhead.

Elevation change: This ride starts at an elevation of 2,600 feet and drops 320 feet as it begins. When you reach the peak of the last knob on Wilson Ridge Trail, you will go back to 2,520 feet before descending the sweet single track to F.R. 4068 and an elevation of 2,360 feet. You will drop to a low elevation of 2,160 feet at the gate at F.R. 45. The climb back to the parking area gains 440 feet, the majority of which is in the last half mile. On the upper loop of this ride, you will drop only 100 feet before regaining that 100 feet on F.R. 45 to reach the 2,600-foot mark. It's then a gradual drop on a grassy double track to the intersection with Woodruff Trail. On this trail, you will descend to 2,530 feet in 0.1 mile. It is a gradual climb to 2,600 feet to reach the parking lot. Total elevation gain is 1,040 feet.

Configuration: Loop

Fall is a good time to check out the area's forest-service roads.

L ocal mountain bikers call the upper part of Wilson Ridge Trail "Twenty-one Jumps" because it starts with a number of "whoop-te-dos" that will make you feel like you're riding a roller coaster. You may be too busy concentrating on the best line in the trail to count the jumps, but you can assume the locals are pretty close in their assessment.

After passing over the "twenty-one jumps," you will travel on a single-track trail for 1.8 miles. At that point, you will come to a very steep, eroded hill, where you will have to push your bike uphill. It will be worth the effort because the crest of Wilson Ridge opens up to offer some striking views of the surrounding mountains.

After a short descent, you turn onto F.R. 4068, which is officially closed to vehicles from January 1 to August 31. You will travel on the gated section of this rolling dirt road for 3.2 miles.

When you loop back to the parking area, you have the option of extending your route by riding on a short section of Woodruff Ridge Trail. A loop on this grassy logging road will extend your trip another 1.5 miles. The sweet surface and great views make the extension worthwhile.

These trails were blazed by members of the High Country Mountain Bike Association. The association is not as active as it was when the first edition was written, so trail maintenance is not as consistent. The trails are fairly well maintained. The one exception is the eroded hill where you have to carry your bike for approximately 0.1 mile.

0.0 Go around the metal guardrail gate located at the far end of the parking area. After entering a clearing, immediately make a sharp right onto a trail that passes over two dirt tank traps.

0.2 Descend on this single-track trail as it passes over the "twenty-one jumps" in the trail.

0.7 You will start a 0.1-mile ascent.

0.9 Continue straight, passing a single-track trail on the left.

1.1   Bear left as you pass a single-track trail on the right.

1.6   You will climb for 0.2 mile.

1.8   Bear left, passing a single-track trail on the right, which is blocked by a large tree. You will come to a very steep, eroded hill, where you will have to push your bike uphill.

1.9   At the crest of the mountain, you will see some beautiful views on the right. The trail starts to descend this mountain.

2.4   Turn right at the metal gate to reach F.R. 4068, a rolling, dirt road. **Note:** this road is officially closed to vehicles from January 1 through August 31. Use caution and watch for cars.

3.2   Continue straight on F.R. 4068. You will pass School House Ridge Trail (# 279), a single track on the left.

4.2   Pass a recent clear-cut area on the right.

5.6   You will pass the metal gate that blocks the other end of F.R. 45 from January through August. Turn right to stay on F.R. 45.

6.7   You will start one last climb.

7.2   The parking area where you started is on the right. This is where you can decide to extend the trip by riding Woodruff Ridge Trail. If you decide on the extension, continue of F.R. 45 and follow the rest of the directions.

8.1   Turn right onto F.R. 4081. There is a plastic trail marker that reads "Woodruff Trail #256" at the intersection of F.R. 4081 and F.R. 45.

8.2   Pass through a white metal gate to continue straight on F.R. 4081, a grassy logging road.

Picking the high line

9.0 You will make a 90-degree, right-hand turn off the grassy logging road onto Woodruff Ridge Trail, where you will start to descend. You will see a tree blazed with red dots and a directional sign for Woodruff Ridge Trail at this turnoff.

9.1 Bear right at the trail intersection.

9.2 Cross a small ditch. There are remains of an old log bridge here.

9.5 Turn left onto F.R. 45 to head back toward the parking lot.

9.7 Turn left into the parking area where you started the ride.

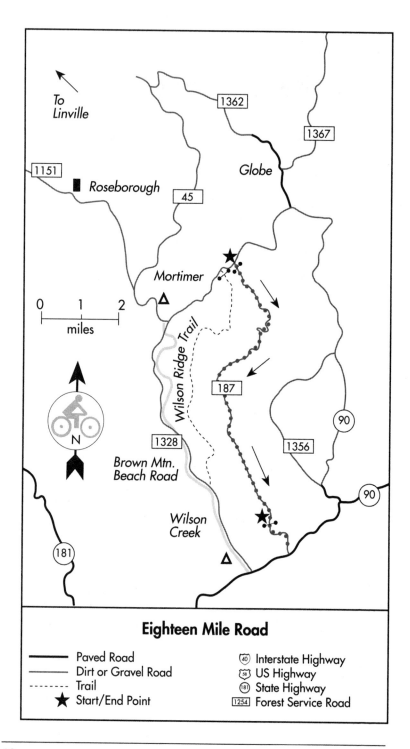

To
Linville

1362

1367

1151

Globe

■ Roseborough

45

Mortimer

△

Wilson Ridge Trail

0   1   2
miles

N

187

1328

Brown Mtn.
Beach Road

1356

90

90

Wilson
Creek

△

181

Eighteen Mile Road

——— Paved Road
——— Dirt or Gravel Road
------- Trail
★ Start/End Point

(40) Interstate Highway
(58) US Highway
(181) State Highway
[1254] Forest Service Road

Eighteen Mile Road Ride

Distance: 18.8 miles

Difficulty: Moderate

Riding surface: Dirt-and-gravel road

Maps: 1. Pisgah National Forest: Grandfather District
2. Wilson Creek Area Trail Map
3. USGS 7.5 minute quadrangle, Collettsville, N.C.
4. USGS 7.5 minute quadrangle, Globe, N.C.
5. Outdoor Recreation Map and Guide, Boone, N.C., region, from Blue Planet Publishing, Inc., P.O. Box 9195, Boone, N.C. 28608

Access: To reach the Roseborough access, drive south on U.S. 221 from the intersection of U.S. 221 and N.C. 105 in Linville. After approximately 0.2 mile, turn left onto Roseborough Road (S.R. 1511) at the four-way stop; this is the second left after the intersection of U.S. 221 and N.C. 105. Roseborough Road is paved for 1.6 miles until it changes to dirt when it reaches the Blue Ridge Parkway. Drive 8.8 miles until you reach the T-intersection with S.R. 90. Turn right and drive 2 miles to Mortimer Recreation Area. Continue on S.R. 90 for about 3.5 miles to the intersection with F.R. 187. There is a sign directing you to Maple Grove Baptist Church at this intersection. The church itself is 0.7 mile from the intersection. Park at any pull-off.

To reach the lower access, follow the above directions to Mortimer Recreation Area. Turn onto Brown Mountain Beach Road (S.R. 1328) and drive about 8.5 miles to the

The views are great from F.R. 187.

end of the road. Turn left onto Adako Road (S.R. 1337), a paved road. After about 1.3 miles, turn left onto Murphy Place Road (S.R. 1407). At times, the road sign designating Murphy Place Road has been missing, so watch your mileage carefully. Drive 1 mile to F.R. 187, which is on the right. This gated forest-service road is officially closed from January through August, but it is frequently left open. Leave your vehicle at any pull-off near this intersection.

Elevation change: The elevation at the beginning of the ride is 2,200 feet. It drops for the majority of the ride, though there are a few steep climbs thrown in to make you feel like you've earned all that downhill. The total elevation gain is 600 feet.

Configuration: One-way

Thrill seekers may scoff at a day spent mountain biking a forest-service road, but this gated dirt road offers a thrill that no single track can match. And that is speed. There are no tight, off-camber, hairpin turns to slow you down, no logs to jump, no sections so steep and technical that you have to stop and pray before plunging headfirst into a green abyss. This road is officially closed from January 1 to August 31 each year, but it has not been closed for the last several years. Without question, single-track trails are great. What mountain biker doesn't love them? But there is no way that you can clock the same speed on a trail that you can on a wildly descending, dirt road.

This particular forest-service road also offers exceptional scenery. It snakes through dense deciduous forests highlighted by occasional patches of evergreens. Flowering trees—Carolina silverbells, dogwoods, and Fraser magnolias—embellish the highland woods during late spring. Mountain creeks sing off in the distance, and a range of wildflowers colorfully dots the hills.

A variety of animals also live in these woods. Grouse, squirrels, wild turkeys, black bear, and white-tailed deer are some

Bluets are common along moist creek banks in the spring.

of the critters you might see slipping through the forest. At some point, you will probably see a tree blazed with three orange marks. These are black-bear sanctuary markers.

The road traces ridge lines for most of its distance, winding to scenic overlooks created by loggers. On clear days, you can see for miles across the valleys and gaps to distant knobs, hills, and mountains. Whatever your politics are on the issue of logging in national forests, you will have to concede that logging activities do clear good views.

It should also be noted that the route of this ride is easy to follow. Simply get on F.R. 187 and stay on it for the entire length.

0.0 After leaving a shuttle vehicle at the lower end of F.R. 187, begin pedaling at the intersection of S.R. 90 and F.R. 187. Turn onto the dirt-and-gravel F.R. 187.

0.6 Bear left past the gated logging road on the right. S.R. 1385 (Maple Tree Place) also branches off to the right here.

Keep yourself and your dog well hydrated.

0.7 Maple Grove Church is on the left. You will pass several houses along this stretch of the road.

1.6 Pass a gated logging road on the left. Stay on the dirt-and-gravel road.

1.8 Pass through a white metal gate. If this gate is open, expect to encounter vehicles on this road. The gate is officially supposed to be closed 8 months of the year. If it is closed, just pedal around it.

2.9 Crest the hill. On the left is a great view of the mountains and the valley below.

3.6 Bear left, passing a gated logging road on the right.

3.8 Pass another gated road on the right.

8.0 There is a nice view on the left.

12.4 Bear right, passing a gated logging road on the left.

14.9 There is a gated logging road that intersects F.R. 187 from the right. Continue on the dirt-and-gravel F.R. 187.

16.4 There is an overlook on the left that allows you to see the results of much of the logging activity in this area.

18.4 You will come to a white metal gate that may be closed eight months of the year. If it is closed, pedal around it. This is the bottom end of F.R. 187.

18.8 Arrive at the intersection with Murphy Place Road. This marks the end of the ride.

Northwest North Carolina

Pisgah National Forest: Linville Gorge Area

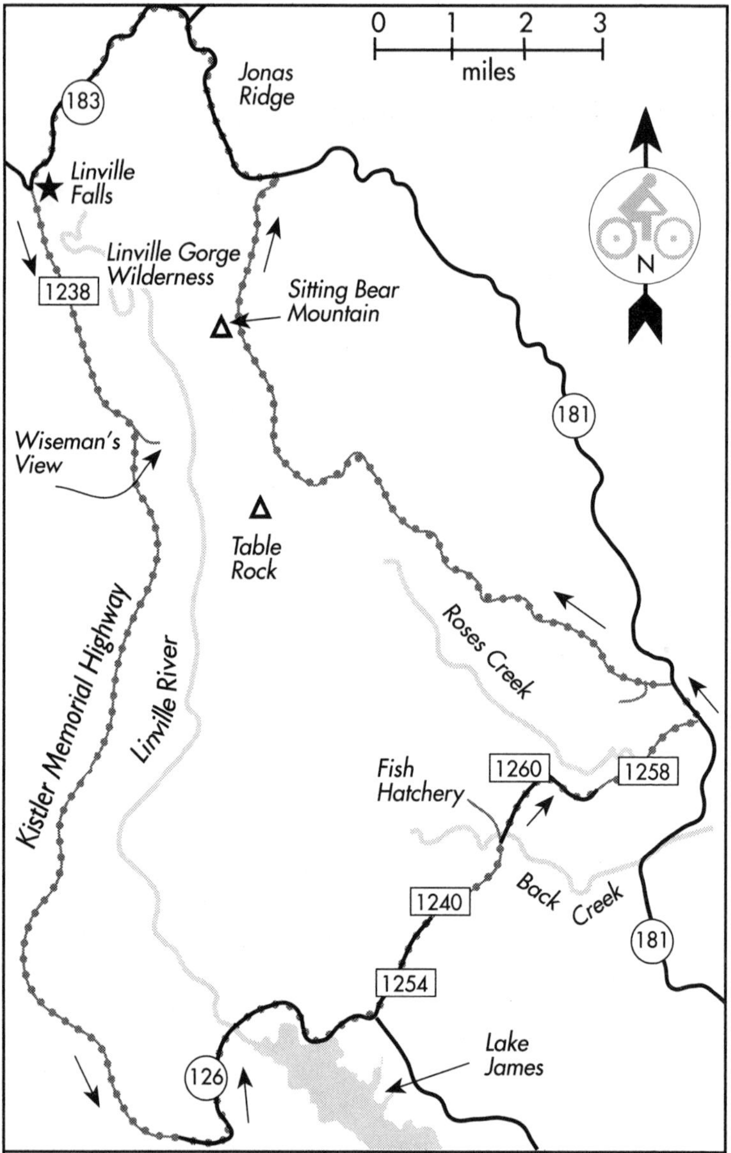
0 1 2 3
miles
Jonas Ridge
183
Linville Falls
Linville Gorge Wilderness
1238
Sitting Bear Mountain
N
181
Wiseman's View
Table Rock
Kistler Memorial Highway
Linville River
Roses Creek
Fish Hatchery
1260
1258
1240
Back Creek
181
1254
Lake James
126

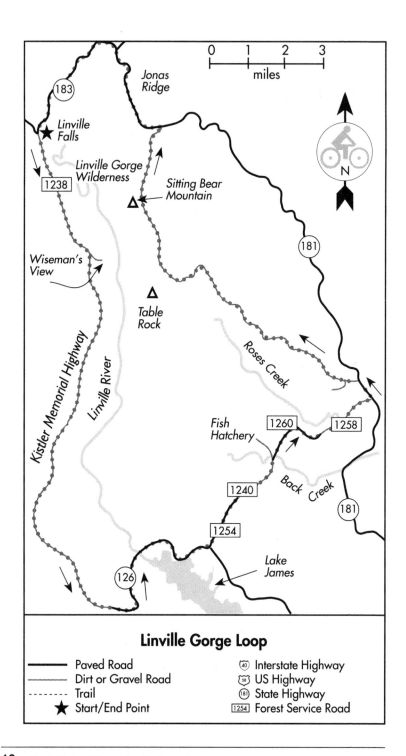

Linville Gorge Loop

Paved Road
Dirt or Gravel Road
Trail
★ Start/End Point
Interstate Highway
US Highway
State Highway
Forest Service Road

Linville Gorge Loop

Distance: 49 miles

Difficulty: Extremely strenuous

Riding surface: Dirt roads, paved roads

Maps: 1. Pisgah National Forest: Grandfather District
2. USGS 7.5 minute quadrangle, Linville Falls, N.C.
3. USGS 7.5 minute quadrangle, Ashford, N.C.
4. USGS 7.5 minute quadrangle, Oak Hill, N.C.
5. USGS 7.5 minute quadrangle, Chestnut Mountain, N.C.

Access: From U.S. 221 in the town of Linville Falls, turn onto N.C. 183 and drive 0.7 mile to the turnoff to the Linville Falls parking area. Park in this unpaved lot.

Elevation change: The ride begins at an elevation of about 3,300 feet at the Linville Falls parking area. It reaches a maximum of 3,950 feet on Kistler Memorial Highway (S.R. 1238) before dropping to 3,550 feet at the turnoff to Wiseman's View. The road drops to 3,000 feet and climbs to 3,400 feet before the final descent to N.C. 126 begins; by the time Kistler Memorial Highway intersects the paved road, the elevation drops to 1,400 feet. Next, the ride drops to 1,200 feet before climbing to 1,300 feet at the intersection with Fish Hatchery Road (C.R. 1254). It then drops to 1,150 feet at the N.C. 181 turnoff. From that point, the dirt road steadily climbs up to and past Table Rock Picnic Area until it reaches 3,600 feet at the Gingercake community. At N.C. 181, the elevation drops to 3,450 feet.

Another climb follows, this time to 3,800 feet. The last few miles of the ride are on a descending grade, as N.C. 183 drops back to the Linville Falls parking area. There is one final 100-foot gain between the Linville River Bridge and the Old N.C. 105 turnoff. The total elevation gain is 4,050 feet.

Configuration: Loop

Nearly 50 incredibly strenuous miles long, this mountain-bike ride is the longest and toughest described in this guidebook. When rating the difficulty of various rides, this one goes out of the ballpark. Without a doubt, this challenging loop is sure to peg the needle of your endurance meter.

Though the miles alone are enough to qualify this ride as strenuous, the challenge doesn't stop with distance. There are quite a few hills to tackle, to the tune of more than 4,000 feet of elevation gain. Even if you are strong, young, and a high-gear snob, you will never make it up some of these steep hills without some serious low-ring action.

And then there are the downhills. These descents are not just technical, they are scary. If you are faint of heart, weak of knee, or short on braking power, you will never make it. Sharp, screaming turns on steep grades combined with extremely technical surfaces make a recipe for a wipeout if ever there was one. Though adrenaline junkies will find it thrilling, some of you will have white-knuckle grips on your brake levers as you negotiate these drops.

There are occasional easy drifts in the ride that will give you a chance to catch your breath before the next punch. These respites may keep you from hurling your bike and yourself into the gorge, but it's the steep stuff you will remember when the ride is over.

If you can hang in there, the rewards are great, for this mountain-bike ride is as beautiful as it is difficult. The route winds around the perimeter of the Linville Gorge Wilderness, with numerous overlooks along the way affording spectacular views. Linville Gorge is formed by Linville Mountain on the west and Jonas Ridge on the east. The ride consists of dirt roads flanking the gorge and a few brief sections of paved road connecting the eastern and western legs of the loop. Even if you normally kick and scream when you have to pedal paved roads on your mountain bike, you will never be happier than when you see blacktop on this ride. After grinding up the tough hills and negotiating the steep descents on the dirt roads, you may find yourself dropping to your knees and kissing the asphalt.

Slicing through this splendid wild country is the pristine Linville River, which thunders for 14 white, riotous miles through the gorge. It drops several thousand feet before finally calming down and draining into Lake James. The Cherokees called the river *Eeseeoh*, meaning "river of many cliffs." As you gaze at the rugged, sheer cliffs soaring 1,000 feet from the lush, green basin of the river, *Eeseeoh* will indeed seem a perfectly appropriate name.

Tucked within this canyon are pockets of virgin forest, some of the few remaining in the United States. These areas are so inaccessible that early timber speculators couldn't take trees

Views of the walls of Linville Gorge are great from Kistler Memorial Highway.

from the backwoods coves. Axes and saws could be brought in, but the loggers had no way to haul out their woody spoils. Then, in 1951, the prospect of future timber harvesting ended when the Linville Gorge was designated a Wilderness Area. Later, this area became one of the original regions covered by the National Wilderness Act. These 7,600 acres are now forever protected. As stated in the act, the Linville Gorge is among those areas "where the earth and its community of life are untrammeled by man, where man himself is a visitor who does not remain." Amen.

Mountain bikes are strictly prohibited in designated Wilderness Areas, but with the aid of the dirt roads skirting the rim of the gorge, cyclists can at least steal a peek into the basin. As you pedal, you will have views of such highlights as Table Rock Mountain, which was used by the Cherokees as a site for their sacred ceremonies. You will also enjoy a view of Hawksbill Mountain, considered by many to be more striking than Table Rock Mountain. Another highlight is Wiseman's View, named for Lafayette "Uncle Fete" Wiseman. This spot on the canyon rim was supposedly one of his favorite campsites for grazing his cattle in the mountain grasses many years ago. Another popular site is Lettered Rock Ridge, located near the turnoff to Table Rock on the eastern edge of the gorge. As the story goes, the marks on the rock are Indian letters painted by the Cherokees in the late 1700s.

Even without these highlights, the beauty of this ride would still take your breath away. Glistening green rhododendron leaves color the edges of the winding dirt roads year-round. The bushes are especially scenic in the summer, when they are heavy with pale pink blossoms.

Autumn rides in the mountains are memorable, with crisp air stirring the brightly colored leaves of the ridge-top hardwoods and finally bringing that long-awaited chill to your bare arms. And of course, there is nothing like gazing up at an autumn sky so blue that it makes you wince.

If you pedal this route on a blustery spring day, you will probably never forget it. As winds blow across the canyon walls, the resulting roar across the mountaintops is incredible.

Kistler Memorial Highway descends to Lake James.

The four-wheel-drive requirements of these dirt roads weed out Sunday drivers and dramatically reduce your chance of encountering passing vehicles. Though this is good for the sake of solitude, you are on your own if you have a mechanical breakdown or an injury or run out of food or water. This is a long, difficult ride without any sag vehicles or stores along the way to assist you. You need to be prepared with ample water and food to last all day. Your bike needs to be in good shape, with well-adjusted, fresh brake pads. If your brakes are beginning to get a little thin, replace them before you head for this ride. You'll be glad that you did. A tool kit and a first-aid kit are also essential. This is an all-day ride, so you will need to get an early start. But most of all, don't overestimate your abilities and physical conditioning. If you are not physically up to this ride, you may find out the hard way that natural selection is still alive and well and hard at work in these hills.

0.0   Begin cycling up Kistler Memorial Highway, a dirt-and-gravel road.

0.4   There is an information center on the right; continue straight.

3.8   F.R. 458 is on the left. This 0.3-mile dirt road leads to Wiseman's View. (See the Wiseman's View Ride for a description of this overlook.)

5.7   There are good views of the walls of the gorge on the left.

7.3   You will hit a brief paved section of road.

12.7   There is an excellent view of Lake James on the left.

13.6   You will cycle through a community of small houses. Where there are country houses, there are also dogs, so watch out.

Table Rock Mountain looms over a peaceful farm setting.

14.0   Paddy Creek Road (S.R. 1237) is to the right; continue straight.

15.5   You will arrive at a stop sign at the intersection of Kistler Memorial Highway and N.C. 126, a paved road. Turn left onto N.C. 126. After the dirt-road workout, the smooth surface and downhill grade of this paved leg of the loop will look like heaven.

17.9   You will pedal across a one-lane bridge over the Linville River. Expect to see a flannel-clad trout fisherman or two planted in the cold water.

19.3   Lake James is on the right. There are some good picnic and resting spots here.

20.4   Turn left onto Fish Hatchery Road, a paved road.

21.0   You will arrive at a Y-intersection. Pea Ridge Road bears right, while Fish Hatchery Road continues straight, changing to a dirt surface and becoming C.R. 1240. To continue the loop, descend on C.R. 1240.

23.5   You will pedal across a one-lane bridge over a creek. Table Rock Mountain is visible to the left across a field.

23.7   You will arrive at a Y-intersection. Bear right on Fish Hatchery Avenue (C.R. 1260), a paved road. Do not bear left on C.R. 1240.

24.8   You will cycle past Mountain Grove United Methodist Church, established in 1860.

25.2   Turn left onto Rose Creek Road (F.R. 1258), a gravel road.

26.3   You will pedal across a one-lane bridge over Rose Creek.

Make sure that you are in good shape or these hills will get you.

27.3 Turn left onto N.C. 181, a paved road.

28.1 Turn left onto Simpson Creek Road (C.R. 1263), a gravel road.

28.3 Turn right at the Table Rock Picnic Area sign.

37.4 Table Rock Picnic Area is on the left at F.R. 210-B; continue straight.

41.9 You will enter the Gingercake community.

42.8 You will arrive at a yield sign; continue straight.

43.1 Turn left onto N.C. 181, a paved road.

45.1 Turn left onto Buckeye Hollow Road.

45.2 Turn left onto S.R. 1267, a dirt road.

46.9 Turn left onto N.C. 183, a paved road.

47.9 You will pass under the Blue Ridge Parkway.

48.4 You will pedal over the Linville River Bridge.

48.9 Turn left onto Old N.C. 105.

49.0 You will arrive back at the starting point at the Linville Falls parking area.

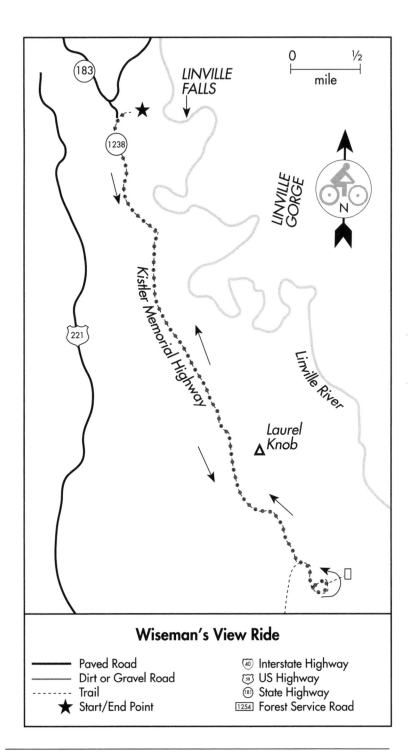

0 ――――― **½**
mile

LINVILLE
FALLS

183

1238

LINVILLE
GORGE

221

Kistler Memorial Highway

Linville River

Laurel
△ Knob

Wiseman's View Ride

―――――― Paved Road
――――― Dirt or Gravel Road
--------- Trail
★ Start/End Point

🔴 Interstate Highway 40
🔴 US Highway 58
🔴 State Highway 181
1254 Forest Service Road

Wiseman's View Ride

Distance: 8.2 miles

Difficulty: Moderate

Riding surface: Dirt road

Maps: 1. Pisgah National Forest: Grandfather District
2. USGS 7.5 minute quadrangle, Linville Falls, N.C.

Access: From U.S. 221 in the town of Linville Falls, turn onto N.C. 183 and drive 0.7 mile to the marked turnoff to the Linville Falls parking area. Park in this unpaved parking lot to begin.

Elevation change: The ride begins at an elevation of 3,300 feet at the Linville Falls parking area. It gains elevation slowly at the beginning, then rapidly intensifies. You will reach a maximum of 3,950 feet before the turnoff to Wiseman's View. The elevation drops to 3,400 feet by the time you reach the parking loop at Wiseman's View. The return trip involves a climb back up to 3,950 feet before the ride drops to 3,300 feet at the starting point. The total elevation gain is 1,200 feet.

Configuration: Out-and-back

View of Table Rock through the trees

olks claim that on dark nights in these mountains, they occasionally see flickering lights darting and dancing on the hills of Brown Mountain. These lights, which have aroused curiosity for hundreds of years, were written about as long ago as the late 1700s by Gerard de Brahm, the first white man to explore this region. Indian mythology also makes mention of the mysterious Brown Mountain Lights.

The most-repeated legend explaining the lights was passed on by a Civil War veteran who served under Robert E. Lee. The soldier told of a low-country planter who became lost while hunting in the mountains. A worried slave came to the hills to try to find him and was seen searching for the man for many days. He even continued his search at night by lantern light. As the legend goes, the old slave died without ever finding his master, but his ghost still searches, and the light from the lantern still glows. Who was this Civil War veteran given credit for passing down the legend through the years? It was Lafayette Wiseman, the man for whom Wiseman's View is named.

When you pedal up to the overlook and gaze across the wilderness from Wiseman's View Trail, you will see the same view that Lafayette Wiseman saw so many years ago. Brown Mountain is visible, of course, as well as the sharply contoured Hawksbill Mountain and Table Rock Mountain. And even though you can't see it, the Linville River thunders for 14 miles through the wilderness, dropping nearly 2,000 feet in a rushing torrent of white water. It slices through the wild, rugged gorge, pinched between sheer rock walls rising high above it.

If the sights from Wiseman's View don't take your breath away, it's probably because there's no breath left in your lungs after the strenuous climb to the overlook. Simply because it sticks to dirt roads for its entire length does not mean that this is a cream-puff tour. Get ready, because this is a fairly tough mountain-bike ride. The climbs are straight-up grinds, and the descents are amazingly difficult. The surface of the road is extremely technical, due to moguls, deep ruts, and holes nearly deep enough to bury bodies. The turns are tight and sharp and will have you squeezing your brakes for all they're worth. You single-track purists might change your mind about dirt-road mountain biking after pedaling this baby.

Mountain bikes are strictly prohibited in the Linville Gorge Wilderness, but this ride offers incredible bird's-eye views of the gorge from the dirt roads along the canyon's rim. As far as scenery goes, it just doesn't get much better than this. The ride weaves through a gorgeous green setting of huge rhododendron thickets, mature hardwoods, and pines. You won't know what to expect around the next bend in the road. Pedaling through these remote backwoods tends to make you feel like you are all alone. But remember, this road is open to traffic. Be alert at all times for passing vehicles, particularly on the sharp turns when descending.

Some portions of the road are adorned with oak trees whose limbs lace together. In winter, the branches look like the arthritic hands of a wispy old woman. In summer, they provide a leafy canopy of blessed shade.

Regardless of the time of year you cycle this trail, you are sure to find beautiful highlights. Spring decorates the forest with blooming dogwoods and the brilliant orange blossoms of flame azaleas. The summer forest is scrubbed in pale pink from rosebay rhododendron blossoms. Autumn is a celebration of vibrant oranges, yellows, and reds that seem to set the forest on fire. And winter soothes the eyes with the clean beauty of slender, gray, leafless hardwood trunks rising amid dark evergreens.

0.0 Begin cycling Kistler Memorial Highway (S.R. 1238), a dirt-and-gravel road.

0.4 An information center is on the right; continue straight.

0.8 There is a large parking area on the left at the Pine Gap trailhead; continue straight. Don't forget that Linville Gorge Wilderness is off-limits to mountain bikes. If you stray from the dirt road onto any of the single-track trails

Pedaling a gentle section of Kistler Memorial Highway

leading down into the gorge, you'll go straight to hell when you die. Don't say you weren't warned.

1.5   There is a parking area on the left at a single-track trailhead; continue straight.

1.6   A pretty view of the gorge is on the left; continue straight.

1.7   A pull-off and overlook of the gorge are on the left; continue straight.

1.9   There is a parking area on the left at the Cabin trailhead; continue straight.

2.4   You will begin a very technical descent.

2.7   There is a parking area on the left at the Babel Tower trailhead; continue straight.

3.8   Turn left onto F.R. 458, a pine-bordered dirt road leading to Wiseman's View.

4.1   You will arrive at the parking loop for Wiseman's View. The 0.2-mile Wiseman's View Trail is for hikers only; mountain bikes are prohibited on it. After taking in the views, turn around and begin retracing your path.

4.4   Turn right onto Kistler Memorial Highway.

8.2   You will arrive back at the starting point at the Linville Falls parking area.

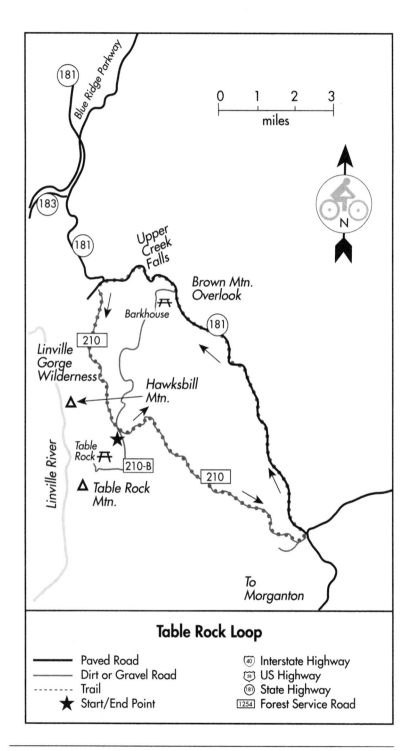

181

Blue Ridge Parkway

183

181

Upper
Creek
Falls

Brown Mtn.
Overlook

Barkhouse

181

0 1 2 3
miles

N

210

Linville
Gorge
Wilderness

Hawksbill
Mtn.

△

Table
Rock

Linville River

210-B

△ Table Rock
Mtn.

210

To
Morganton

Table Rock Loop

——— Paved Road   ⓐ Interstate Highway
——— Dirt or Gravel Road   ⓢ US Highway
- - - - Trail   ⑱ State Highway
★ Start/End Point   1254 Forest Service Road

Table Rock Loop

Distance: 26.2 miles

Difficulty: Strenuous

Riding surface: Dirt road, paved road

Maps: 1. Pisgah National Forest: Grandfather District
2. USGS 7.5 minute quadrangle, Linville Falls, N.C.
3. USGS 7.5 minute quadrangle, Chestnut Mountain, N.C.
4. USGS 7.5 minute quadrangle, Oak Hill, N.C.

Access: From the intersection of N.C. 181 and N.C. 183 south of Linville, drive south on N.C. 181 for approximately 3 miles to the turnoff for Gingercake Road (S.R. 1264); there is a sign at this turnoff showing the mileage to Table Rock Picnic Area. Turn right and drive 0.3 mile to a fork in the road. Bear left on Gingercake Acres Road, which becomes F.R. 210; the road changes from pavement to dirt. Drive 5.4 miles to the turnoff to Table Rock Picnic Area at F.R. 210-B. You can either park at a pull-off near this intersection or drive nearly 3 miles up F.R. 210-B to Table Rock Picnic Area and park there. Since there is limited parking at the picnic area, it is best to park elsewhere on pretty weekends, when the area is heavily used. Starting at the picnic area adds about 6 miles to the ride.

Elevation change: The ride begins at an elevation of 2,600 feet at the intersection of F.R. 210 and F.R. 210-B. It descends to 1,150 feet by the turnoff for N.C. 181. Then the climbing begins. You will pedal to an elevation of 3,450 feet by the turnoff for Gingercake Road and reach a maximum of 3,600 feet within the next mile. You will lose about 1,000 feet in the next 4 miles back to the starting point. The total elevation gain is 2,450 feet.

Configuration: Loop

Hills, hills, and more hills . . .

It's either up or down on this ride, with very few level spots in between. Starting off with a descent, you will bomb down a beautiful forest-service road that winds through dense forests of white pine, spruce, and oak. Occasional flashes of silver will grab your attention, as sparkling mountain streams trickle through basins filled with hemlock and rhododendron. The scenery is gorgeous and the descent is thrilling, but there is work to do. Fighting gravity is a tough job, but somebody's got to do it. And the task begins on N.C. 181.

This is a monster climb—2,300 feet of elevation gain in a measly 11 miles. But it could be worse. The paved surface makes the climbing constant, with no interruptions—like a washboard surface or potholes—to mess up your rhythm. Technical expertise is not required to crest this climb, but endurance and strength are essential. This is a great transition loop for experienced road cyclists interested in trying on a mountain bike for size. The paved portion of road is steep, but the extra gears on a mountain bike help a lot.

For some cyclists, hill climbing is a head game, a sort of Zen experience. Steady pedaling seems to free you of the petty distractions of everyday life. You forget about the proposal you have to make next Thursday; you forget about the weird pinging sound your car engine started making last week; you forget about the bills piling up on your desk. For now, you are only aware of the flickering specks of granite flowing beneath your slowly rolling front wheel and the burning of your quads. If you need a mantra for these hills, pick up Luka Bloom's *Acoustic Motorbike* CD and cue it up to the title song. The tune and chorus are sure to surface in your mind on long hauls like these.

As the miles and hours pile up, you will need to stop and refuel. Bonking is a distinct certainty if you don't replace spent carbohydrates along the way. Be sure to pack sports bars, fig bars, or other snacks, and eat them before you start getting hungry. There are some inviting places along the way to stop if you need the rest—Brown Mountain Overlook, Barkhouse Picnic Area, and Upper Creek Falls, to name a few. If you can spare the energy, you can also take a round-trip hike of about a mile and a half to Upper Creek Falls; the trail is for foot travel only, so lock up your bike and hoof it.

The climbing ends, as all climbing does. Fueled with the knowledge that the work is over, you will make a swift descent on the winding dirt road that leads back to Table Rock. You'll be exhausted and drained, yet mildly giddy.

There is something about these strenuous rides that keeps us coming back for more. Maybe it's the sense of accomplishment that draws us back. Maybe it's the rush of endorphins we get from extended aerobic exercise. Or maybe it's just the thought of a cold beer buried in a cooler of crushed ice. Whatever the source, you know the feeling. And it's awfully good.

Heavily forested dirt roads are perfect for mountain-bike rides.

0.0 From the intersection of F.R. 210 and F.R. 210-B (which leads to Table Rock Picnic Area), begin cycling south on F.R. 210.

9.1 Turn left onto Simpson Creek Road (C.R. 1263), a gravel road.

9.3 Turn left onto N.C. 181, a paved road.

9.5 Brown Mountain Beach Road (S.R. 1328) is on the right; continue straight.

10.6 Steele Creek Park and Campground are on the left; continue straight.

11.2 Daniel Boone Campground is on the right; continue straight.

11.8 You will enter Pisgah National Forest.

18.1 There is a parking area on the right for Upper Creek and Greentown trails; continue straight.

18.6 Barkhouse Picnic Area is on the left.

19.4 Upper Creek Falls is on the right.

19.5 You will leave Pisgah National Forest.

20.5 Gingercake Road is on the left. There is a sign showing the distance to Table Rock Picnic Area (8.5 miles). Turn left here.

20.8 You will come to a fork in the road; bear left onto Gingercake Acres Road, which becomes F.R. 210.

26.2 You will arrive at the turnoff to Table Rock Picnic Area at F.R. 210-B and the starting point.

Northwest North Carolina

Pisgah National Forest: Boone Fork Area

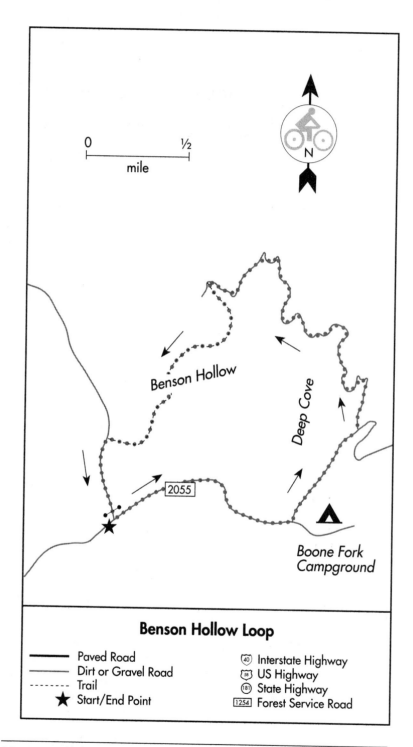

Benson Hollow Loop

▬▬ Paved Road	ⓐ Interstate Highway
▬▬ Dirt or Gravel Road	⑤⑧ US Highway
- - - - Trail	⑱ State Highway
★ Start/End Point	1254 Forest Service Road

Benson Hollow Loop

Distance: 5.4 miles

Difficulty: Easy to moderate

Riding surface: Dirt road, old logging road, single-track trail

Maps: 1. Pisgah National Forest: Grandfather District
2. USGS 7.5 minute quadrangle, Globe, N.C.
3. USGS 7.5 minute quadrangle, Buffalo Cove, N.C.
4. Outdoor Recreation Map and Guide, Boone, N.C., region, from Blue Planet Publishing, Inc., P.O. Box 9195, Boone, N.C. 28608

Access: From Blowing Rock, drive south on U.S. 321 for 13.3 miles. Turn right onto Roby Martin Road (S.R. 1349). After 1.5 miles, the pavement ends and Roby Martin Road becomes a gravel road; continue straight. At 2.5 miles, you will come to a fork; bear right to continue. You will come to a stop sign at 4.2 miles; turn right onto S.R. 1368, a paved road. At 7.2 miles, you will see a sign for Boone Fork Recreation Area; turn right onto F.R. 2055, a dirt road leading to the campground. There is a gated road on the left at 1 mile; park at any nearby pull-off. Do not block the gate.

Elevation change: The ride begins at an elevation of about 1,250 feet and gradually climbs to 1,400 feet at Boone Fork Campground. It gains an additional 200 feet on the logging road before beginning to drop on the single-track trail. At the dirt road near the end of the loop, the elevation drops to 1,350 feet. It continues to drop, finally reaching

Streams and creeks are numerous in the Boone Fork area.

1,250 feet at the starting point. The total elevation gain is 350 feet.

Configuration: Loop

Are you tired of old man winter's frosty fingers stroking the back of your neck? Are you sick of pulling on layer after layer of polypro and pile before hitting the trails? Are you unable to stand one more ride so cold that you have to wiggle into those bulky winter gloves that make your fingers as useless as if they were shot up with Novocaine?

As scenic as winter mountain biking is in the high mountains of North Carolina, even the most tolerant cyclist can become a little weary of the frigid temperatures. But there's a lovely area south of Boone and Blowing Rock that is substantially warmer than the high-elevation hills. Welcome to Boone Fork.

When blustery winds and subfreezing temperatures prevail in the northern reaches of Pisgah, the rides in the Boone Fork area hold great appeal for cyclists. The elevation difference of several thousand feet remarkably affects the mercury in thermometers. Also, the low-lying hollows in this area tend to hang onto the warmth, due to their natural protection from bone-chilling winds. But when summer arrives with its baggage of heat and humidity, mountain bikers take flight and migrate back to the cooler northern hills.

There are a number of ride possibilities in this area of Pisgah National Forest, including this very popular loop. If you pitch a tent in the campground, you can cycle straight from your zippered front door to begin this ride. Dirt roads, single-track trails, climbs, descents, stream crossings, pretty views, beautiful flora—this loop offers just about everything that a mountain biker could want, *and* at relatively comfortable temperatures.

Your warmup begins on a gradually climbing dirt road leading to Boone Fork Campground. You'll make a left turn onto another dirt road, this one gated and overgrown with green vegetation in the spring and summer. Fraser magnolias, holly, hemlock, and rhododendron grow in the moist soil of the thick deciduous forest flanking the road. Farther up the ridge, deciduous azaleas flourish in the drier, more acidic soil. Spring comes early on this low-elevation loop; expect to see blooms here first.

After turning off the old logging road, you will pedal along a lush, green single-track trail that leads down into Benson Hollow. Once you enter this verdant Eden, you'll feel almost like you are riding through a bowl filled with sunshine. A luxuriant ground cover of turkey feet carpets this low-lying area. Mountain streams sparkle when shafts of sunlight hit their trickling waters, creating a dazzling sight.

Then it's back out of this green glade and onto an open dirt road again. It won't be long until you catch sight of a gate across the road, which, unfortunately, marks the end of the

Mountain biking is great in the Boone Fork area.

ride. **Note:** This ride is a good ride for bikers who want to try single-tracks for the first time.

0.0   From the parking pull-off, cycle up the dirt road leading to the campground.

0.5   You will pass a popular fishing lake on the left.

1.0   You will pedal into Boone Fork Campground. Bear left onto an old logging road and cycle around the gate.

1.5   You will come to a fork in the road; bear left.

2.5   You will pass some single-track trails on your left. Do not take these trails.

3.9   Turn left onto a wide, grassy trail that is marked by orange streamers hanging in some small pine trees. There is a large oak tree on the right, which has logs piled underneath it. There is a pile of old logs on the left as well. You will know you have missed the trail turnoff if the dirt road enters a clear-cut area; the road then swings to the right and its surface changes to grass. The trail you should be following appears to be an old logging road.

4.0   Turn right onto a single-track trail. The old logging road you just left becomes overgrown at this turn, so the single track on the right should be obvious.

4.1   Cross the creek. There are remains of a log bridge on the left. The trail may look like it ends at the creek, but it continues on the other side. In the next 0.5 mile, you will cross the creek an additional four times.

4.6   After crossing the creek, you will walk over some rock ledges on the other side.

4.8   You will cross a cattle guard.

4.9   You will see a National Forest Property Boundary sign.

5.0   Bear left onto a grassy logging road.

5.4   Arrive back at the parking area.

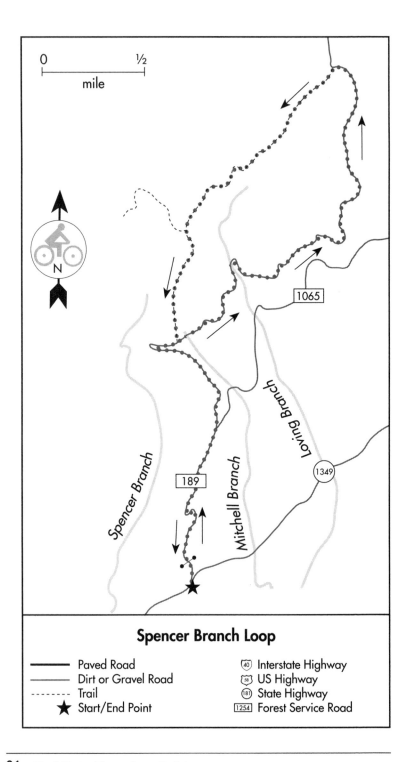

Spencer Branch Loop

——— Paved Road	ⓐ Interstate Highway
——— Dirt or Gravel Road	ⓤ US Highway
- - - - - Trail	⑱ State Highway
★ Start/End Point	⌷1254⌶ Forest Service Road

Spencer Branch Loop

Distance: 8.2 miles

Difficulty: Moderate

Riding surface: Dirt road, single-track trail

Maps: 1. Pisgah National Forest: Grandfather District
   2. USGS 7.5 minute quadrangle, Buffalo Cove, N.C.
   3. USGS 7.5 minute quadrangle, Lenoir, N.C.
   4. Outdoor Recreation Map and Guide, Boone,
      N.C., region, from Blue Planet Publishing, Inc.,
      P.O. Box 9195, Boone, N.C. 28608

Access: From Blowing Rock, drive south on U.S. 321 for 13.3 miles. Turn right onto Roby Martin Road (S.R. 1349). At 1.5 miles, the pavement ends and Roby Martin Road becomes a gravel road; continue straight. At 2.5 miles, you will come to a fork; bear right to continue. Spencer Branch Road (F.R. 189) is on the right at 2.8 miles. Park at any pull-off near the beginning of this dirt road. Do not block the gate.

Elevation change: The ride begins at an elevation of 1,300 feet and steadily climbs to 2,300 feet by the turnoff at the meadow. There are a few more brief climbs, but the ride is mostly descending at this point. Toward the end of the ride, the elevation drops to 1,600 feet at the intersection of the trail and the road. A final drop on the forest-service road returns you to an elevation of 1,300 feet. The total elevation gain is 1,000 feet.

Configuration: Loop

Since the first edition of this guide was published, logging activity along the route has altered the environment considerably. Instead of the dense forest that was described in the earlier version, you will now find clear-cut areas.

Winding up and around the steep-sided ridge lines, this forest-service road will lead you into a remote backwoods setting that is perfect for a mountain bike. The climbing is relentless for about 4 miles, but the views at the top are spectacular.

The Boone Fork area is an especially good mountain-biking destination in the winter, due to its relatively warm temperatures. This loop is located at an elevation several thousand feet lower than Wilson Creek and other northern areas of Pisgah, which tends to nudge temperatures up quite a bit. In fact, this ride's maximum elevation is less than the elevations at the starting points of some rides.

The climbing ends and the fun begins when you pedal into a meadow half-enclosed by a wall of pines. Turning left onto an abandoned jeep track, you will pedal up to a grassy knoll and then down a stretch of single-track trail. Your descent be-

Some of these single-track trails are quite technical.

gins on a narrow path that can barely be seen as it trickles through a riotous tangle of pale green brush. The trail then slips into a forest, where it is protected from being overtaken by undergrowth; the canopy of mature, tall trees filters the sunlight and discourages the growth of understory.

The trail will disappear again, though this time not into briers and brush. The late-autumn leaf drop creates a deep sea of dry, sepia-tinted leaves that obscures the trail.

The rest of the ride is less remarkable, as the descending trail loops back to the dirt road. Exposed roots, small logs, and rocks will require you to make technical moves on some portions of the trail. Other sections are smooth and swift. There are some blowdowns near the end of the trail; you will have to carry your bike around them. Once you pop back onto the dirt road, a right turn will lead you on a fast descent back to the starting point.

0.0 Begin by pedaling around the white metal gate across the road.

0.5 Pass a hiking trail on the right; continue straight.

1.0 A logging road turns off to the right; continue straight.

3.2 On the right are great views of the ridges surrounding this area and the valley below.

3.5 There is a hiking trail on the right; bear left.

4.3 Turn left at the fork in the road. You will enter a meadow at the top of this ridge. At the far side of the meadow, turn left and cross over two dirt tank traps. You will emerge from the meadow onto a grassy double-track trail. Do not take the road directly ahead.

5.7 There is a single-track trail on the right; bear left.

5.9 Start a steep 0.1-mile climb.

Dirt-road riding is ideal for the whole family, including the dog.

6.0   When you reach the top of this ridge, you will have a good view of the mountains before descending.

6.5   Continue straight as you emerge onto a recently graded logging road.

6.7   After crossing a large dirt tank trap, turn right onto Spencer Branch Road. Retrace your route back to the parking area.

8.4   You arrive back at the parking area.

Southwest Virginia
Mount Rogers National Recreation Area

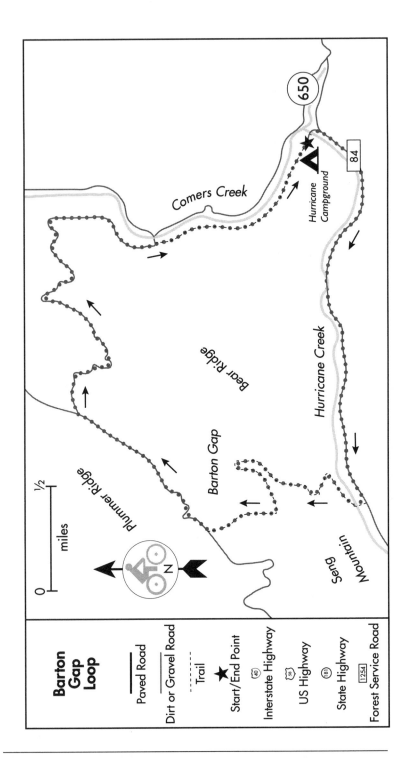

Barton
Gap
Loop

Paved Road
Dirt or Gravel Road
------ Trail
★ Start/End Point
⑩ Interstate Highway
🛡 US Highway
⑱ State Highway
1254 Forest Service Road

Comers Creek

650

84

Hurricane Campground

Hurricane Creek

Bear Ridge

Plummer Ridge

Barton Gap

Seng Mountain

miles

0   ½

N

Barton Gap Loop

Distance: 7.8 miles

Difficulty: Moderate

Riding Surface: Dirt road, single-track trail

Maps: 1. Mount Rogers National Recreation Area Map
2. USGS 7.5 minute quadrangle, Troutdale, Va.
3. USGS 7.5 minute quadrangle, Whitetop Mountain, Va.

Access: From the intersection of U.S. 58 and Va.91, take U.S. 58 East. Drive 9.7 miles to the intersection with Va. 603 at Konnarock. U.S. 58 makes a sharp right here. Continue straight on Va. 603. After 2.9 miles, you will pass Weaver Grocery. Turn right onto Va. 603 when it makes a right turn. Continue on Va. 603 for 7.5 miles to the intersection with Va. 16 at Troutdale. Turn left on Va. 16 and go 2.5 miles. Turn left onto Va. 650 and go 1.4 miles to the Hurricane Campground entrance. F.R. 84 begins at this point. Park on F.R. 84, on the left near the entrance to the campground.

Elevation change: This ride begins at an elevation of 2,700 feet at the Hurricane Campground. It climbs 800 feet to a maximum elevation of 3,500 feet on the Barton Gap Trail, then drops 700 feet to Va. 650. The ride drops another 350 feet to the creek. From the creek, it is then a mere 50-foot gain back to the starting point. Total elevation gain is 850 feet; total elevation drop 1,050 feet.

Configuration: Loop

It is easy to understand why so many mountain bikers consider Mount Rogers National Recreation Area a mecca, especially when you cycle excellent rides such as this loop. Keep your eyes open for deer, turkey, and wildflowers, as they are all plentiful in this area.

Barton Gap Loop is a moderately difficult ride due to the endurance it requires, rather than its technical challenge. This ride starts on F.R. 84, a dirt road. It crosses Hurricane Creek and gently ascends to a ridge. The route then hugs the side of the mountain on a tight single-track trail. The route passes through Barton Gap and continues between Plummer and Bear Ridges before intersecting with F.R. 643, a dirt-and-gravel road. This road is in good condition, with a smooth, hard-packed surface. During autumn, the leaves of the tall hardwood trees bordering the road are absolutely stunning. When the leaves of trees growing at lower elevations down in the Boone area are just beginning to tease you with hint of color, these are already at their peak, with glowing golds, reds, and oranges.

Continue your descent another 3.3 miles to the intersection with Comers Creek. Follow the wide creekside forest trail as it hugs the west bank of Comers Creek. This pretty single-track trail is actually an abandoned railroad grade. It follows a gently ascending course peppered with annoying rocks. Even if you have front suspension, the rocky surface creates a bumpy ride. Without suspension, you'll run a serious risk of having an eyeball or two falling out of socket.

After this last workout, it's out to the main campground for a cold drink of water before returning to where you parked.

0.0   From the pull-off at the Hurricane Campground entrance, start a westward climb on F.R. 84, a dirt road.

2.0   Turn right onto Barton Gap Trail. Please note this trail may be hard to find. There is a placard with an international symbol for a motorcyclist attached to a signpost next to the road at this point. Directly across the road is a hiker-only trail that connects with the Appalachian Trail. The hiker-only trail is designated by a placard with the international symbol for a hiker attached to a sign-post. Immediately after turning onto Barton Gap Trail, you cross Hurricane Creek, which will be a rocky crossing.

2.5 You will start a gentle climb on a narrow single-track trail. There are good views to the right. This section hugs the side of the mountain. There is limited sight distance, so use caution and watch for other trail users.

2.6 The trail becomes more level, before a gentle descent begins.

2.9 You will descend for the next 0.6 mile. There are some rocky sections with a few log crossings.

3.5 At the intersection with F.R. 643, turn right onto F.R. 643 and descend.

4.5 You will start a gradual climb.

4.9 You will pass a metal gate on the right. Continue on the rolling terrain of F.R. 643. Deer are plentiful, so keep your eyes open.

6.8 Turn right onto the trail that parallels Comers Creek. Do not cross the creek.

7.2 Begin a rocky technical section.

7.4 Turn left onto the pavement as you emerge at Hurricane Campground. Water and bathrooms are available for use here. If you plan to use the picnic, camping, or shower facilities, there is a daily fee of $3.

7.8 Pedal past several campsites, through the entrance to the campground, and back onto F.R. 84 to your parking site.

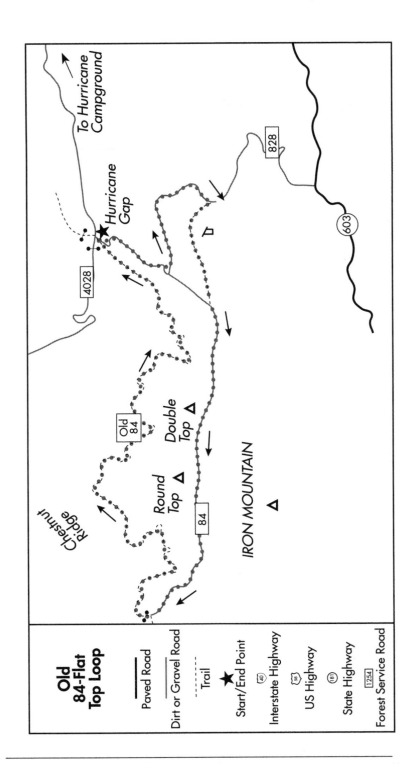

Old 84-Flat Top Loop

- Paved Road
- Dirt or Gravel Road
- Trail
- ★ Start/End Point
- 🛣 Interstate Highway
- 🛣 US Highway
- 🛣 State Highway
- Forest Service Road

To Hurricane Campground

Hurricane Gap

828

603

4028

Old 84

Double Top ▲

Round Top ▲

IRON MOUNTAIN ▲

84

Chestnut Ridge

Old 84 – Flat Top Loop

Distance: 10.4 Miles

Difficulty: Moderate

Riding Surface: Gravel road, single-track trail, grassy double-track trail

Maps: 1. Mount Rogers National Recreation Area
2. USGS 7.5 minute quadrangle, Whitetop Mountain, Va.

Access: From the intersection of U.S. 58 and Va. 91, take U.S. 58 East. Drive 9.7 miles to the intersection with Va. 603 at Konnarock. U.S. 58 makes a sharp right here. Continue straight on Va. 603. After 2.9 miles, you will pass Weaver Grocery. Turn right onto Va. 603 when it makes a right turn. After 4.3 miles, turn left onto F.R. 828, just before the Grindstone Campground. Proceed on F.R. 828 for 1.5 miles until you arrive at a level, grassy field used as a primitive camping area. It is marked with several trees bearing a red number 44. There is plenty of space to park. You will start your ride here.

Elevation change: The elevation at the F.R. 828 starting point is approximately 4,000 feet. The route on Iron Mountain Trail to F.R. 84 climbs 600 feet. It then descends 800 feet to the Old 84 trailhead. The trail ascends to 4,000 feet near Double Top, then drops 200 feet to Hurricane Gap. There is another short climb of 600 feet on F.R. 84 and F.R. 828. This ascent is followed by a descent of 200 feet back to the starting point. Total elevation gain is 1,400 feet; total elevation loss is 1,200 feet.

Configuration: Loop

Pedaling up the grassy double track of Old 84

The ride begins on Iron Mountain Trail, a single track that winds up to Cherry Tree Shelter. After passing the shelter, you will have a short climb on a single track before dropping down to the intersection with F.R. 84.

Turning left onto the dirt-packed F.R. 84, you will start a steep descent. Watch for the turnoff for Old 84. Old 84 used to be the main road until construction of the current F.R. 84. The forest service made good use of the old roadbed by removing the asphalt and seeding the roadbed with grass. It is now one of the most pleasant trails in the area.

Follow Old 84 as it rolls along the mountainside. This is a nicely shaded trail that is an ideal summer ride. When the leaves are off the trees, expect some dazzling views of the opposite ridgeline and the valley below. Old 84 ends when it intersects with the new F.R. 84. You will turn right here and begin a half-mile climb to F.R. 828. You will end the ride with a nice descent to the parking area.

0.0 From the parking area, turn right onto F.R. 828.

0.1 On the left, you will pass a metal gate with blue blazes.

0.3 Turn left onto Iron Mountain Trail. Look for the yellow blaze and the Iron Mountain Trail sign.

0.6 Continue straight on Iron Mountain Trail at Cherry Tree Shelter. There is a directional trail sign on the right, which reads "Straight Branch Shelter 6 miles." Proceed toward Straight Branch Shelter.

1.8 Pass through the bollard gate with a yellow blaze on it.

1.9 Turn left at the intersection with F.R. 84 and descend on this dirt road.

3.7 Turn right off F.R. 84 and go around the metal gate. There is a number 49 painted on the tree here.

Pausing at the Cherry Tree Shelter

3.8 Bear right onto Old 84. Jerry's Creek Trail turns off to the left at this intersection.

5.7 There are some nice views on the left.

6.7 You will come to a clearing on the right, where you will see the number 50 painted on a tree. Continue straight past the clearing on the grassy double track.

7.3 Notice the old-growth hemlock trees on the left. Descend gently on this grassy double track.

7.8 Cross over two dirt berms, or "tank traps."

8.6 Turn right onto Old 84 and begin a short grade to F.R. 84, a dirt road. **Note:** Roland Creek Trail, marked by a metal gate with the number 52 painted on it, intersects from the left. Do not take this trail.

8.8 Turn right at the Old 84 intersection with F.R. 84. Start to climb on F.R. 84.

9.3 At the intersection of F.R. 84 and F.R. 828, turn left onto F.R. 828. You will start a short climb here.

10.0 The road begins to level out, before descending rapidly.

10.4 Arrive back at the starting point.

The forest service made good use of the Old 84 roadbed.

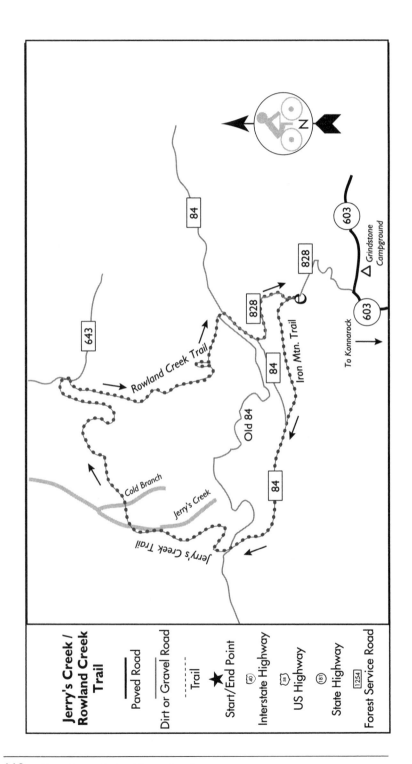

Jerry's Creek / Rowland Creek Trail

- **Paved Road**
- **Dirt or Gravel Road**
- **- - - -** Trail
- ★ Start/End Point
- (40) Interstate Highway
- (58) US Highway
- (16) State Highway
- [1254] Forest Service Road

N

84

643

Rowland Creek Trail

828

828

84

Iron Mtn. Trail

Old 84

84

Cold Branch

Jerry's Creek

Jerry's Creek Trail

603

△ Grindstone Campground

603

To Konnarock

Jerry's Creek /
Rowland Creek Trail *

Distance: 13 miles

Difficulty: Strenuous and technical

Riding Surface: Gravel forest-service road, single-track trail, grassy double-track trail

Maps: 1. Mount Rogers National Recreation Area
2. USGS 7.5 minute quadrangle, Whitetop Mountain, Va.

Access: From the intersection of U.S. 58 and Va. 91, take U.S. 58 East. Drive 9.7 miles to the intersection with Va. 603 at Konnarock. U.S. 58 makes a sharp right here. Continue straight on Va. 603. After 2.9 miles, you will pass Weaver Grocery. Turn right onto Va. 603 when it makes a right turn. After 4.3 miles, turn left onto F.R. 828, just before the Grindstone Campground. Proceed on F.R. 828 for 1.5 miles until you arrive at a level, grassy field used as a primitive camping area. It is marked with several tress bearing a red number 44. There is plenty of space to park. You will start your ride here.

Elevation change: The ride begins at an elevation of approximately 4,000 feet. It then climbs 600 feet on Iron Mountain Trail to F.R. 84, where it descends 800 feet to the Jerry's Creek trailhead. Get ready for the big drop. Jerry's Creek Trail descends 1,000 feet over the next mile on narrow, twisting, single track before reaching the crossing at Jerry's Creek. After the creek crossing, you climb 200 feet

* **Note:** *There are two common spellings for the creek and waterfall mentioned in this chapter. Topographical maps and some trail signs read "Roland Creek." The U.S. Forest Service says the official spelling is "Rowland." We have chosen to use the forest service's spelling.*

and drop 440 feet on a grassy double track before coming to Rowland Creek Trail. Fun time's over. Now you have to climb 1,200 feet over 3 miles to reach the end of Rowland Creek Trail. There is a climb of 600 feet, followed by a descent of 200 feet, before returning to the starting point. Total elevation gain is 2,600 feet; total elevation loss is 2,440 feet.

Configuration: Loop

This ride starts on F.R. 828 then proceeds to the Jerry's Creek / Old 84 trailhead via the twisting, single-track Iron Mountain Trail. The ride on Iron Mountain Trail is a gradual climb until you reach Cherry Tree Shelter. It then descends to the dirt-packed F.R. 84.

When you begin your ride on Jerry's Creek Trail, you will follow the orange blazes which designate the Highlands Horse Trail for most of this ride. At the start of Jerry's Creek Trail, you descend very quickly for the first mile on some very technical, narrow, rocky, off-camber single track that hugs the side of the mountain. Concentrate on your line here because one false move takes you over the side and down the hill. You may also be surprised by some patches of large, embedded rock. You can easily have flat tires on this section, so make sure you have a spare tube and patch kit with you. At the bottom of this technical descent, you cross Jerry's Creek. Proceed on a pleasant grassy double track—a nice reprieve from your harrowing descent.

At the end of Jerry's Creek Trail, you come to F.R. 643. It's just a short jaunt to Rowland Creek Trail, where you would be advised to have your climbing legs warmed up. Some of the steep sections on this trail may cause you to walk your bike, but it's worth it. About halfway up the climb, you will be rewarded with a beautiful view, which looks down the cascading Rowland Falls.

After this reward, you have to climb your way out to the intersection of F.R. 84/Old 84/Rowland Creek Trail. At this intersection, take F.R. 84 and F.R. 828, back to your starting point.

One of the rewards on this trip is a view of Rowland Falls.

0.0 Facing the road from the parking area, turn right onto F.R. 828.

0.1 On the left, you will pass a metal gate with blue blazes on it.

0.3 Turn left onto Iron Mountain Trail. Look for the yellow blaze and an Iron Mountain Trail sign.

0.6 At Cherry Tree Shelter, continue straight on Iron Mountain Trail. There is a directional trail sign reading "Straight Branch Shelter 6 miles." Proceed toward that shelter, following the yellow rectangle blazes.

1.8 Pass through a bollard gate with a yellow blaze on it.

1.9 At the intersection, turn left and descend on F.R. 84, which is a dirt road.

3.7 Turn right off F.R. 84 and go around a metal gate. Several nearby trees have a red number 49 painted on them.

3.8 At the intersection of Old 84 and Jerry's Creek Trail, turn left onto Jerry's Creek Trail. A directional sign reading "Jerry's Creek Trail 643, 5.5 miles" will help you pick the correct trail. The Old 84 trail turns to the right at this point.

4.2 Begin descending on a very rocky single track. This section is narrow and sight distance is limited, so use caution.

4.7 The trail flattens out as you reach the bottom of the descent. Jerry's Creek is on the right.

5.1 Cross Jerry's Creek, following the orange blazes. This section is a rolling, grassy double track.

7.0 Begin descending on the grassy double track. There are some nice views of the opposing ridge line.

8.2 Go around a metal gate. You will see the intersection of F.R. 643 and Jerry's Creek Trail straight ahead.

8.3 Turn right onto F.R. 643.

8.4 Turn right at the sign that reads "Rowland Creek Trail, Falls-1.5, Old 84-3, Loop-10."

8.7 There is a rocky creek crossing. Follow the orange blazes. Notice the rock overhangs and the beautiful scenery of the creek below. Start a gradual, loose rocky climb.

9.4 Cross the creek again. Rowland Creek is now on the right.

9.5 Turn left at the T-intersection. Follow the orange blazes. You will encounter a rocky switchback and a steep technical climb on a single-track trail.

9.8 The trail levels out briefly, before resuming its steep climb.

9.9 You will see Rowland Falls below you to the right. It is possible to scramble down to the creek for a better view and a cool swim. The trail becomes very smooth ahead, but continues to climb.

10.1 Cross the creek.

10.3 There is a rocky creek crossing. You may want to try a possible line to the left. Continue to follow the orange blazes.

10.4 Turn left at the double orange blaze. The number 52 is painted on a tree.

10.6 Continue climbing on the grassy double track. Try to hang in there!

11.3 Go around a metal gate to the intersection with F.R. 84. Turn right at this intersection. You will see Old 84 to the right; continue on the dirt-packed F.R. 84.

11.4 Turn right, following the dirt-packed F.R. 84. You will pass Old 84. F.R. 84 starts to climb.

11.9 At the intersection of F.R. 84 and F.R. 828, turn left onto F.R. 828. There's only one more short climb.

12.6 The road begins to level out, before descending rapidly.

13.0 Arrive back at the starting point.

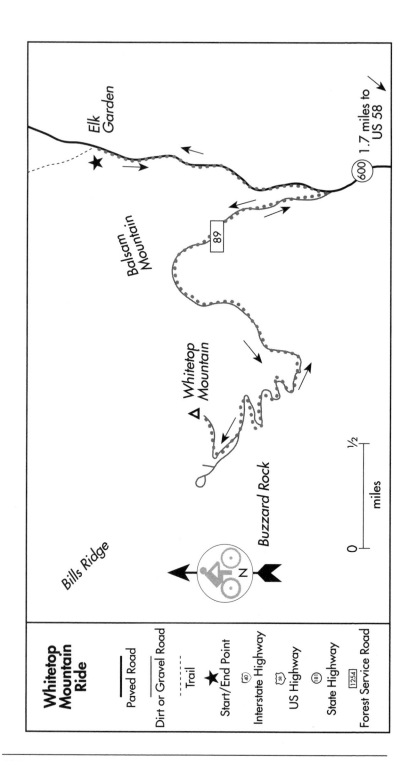

Whitetop Mountain Ride

Distance: 8.2 miles

Difficulty: Moderate

Riding Surface: Dirt-and-gravel road

Maps: 1. Mount Rogers National Recreation Area
2. USGS 7.5 minute quadrangle, Whitetop Mountain, Va.

Access: From the intersection of U.S. 58 and Va. 91, take U.S. 58 East. Drive 9.7 miles to the intersection with Va. 603 at Konnarock. Turn right to stay on U.S. 58. Drive 7.7 miles to the intersection with S.R. 600. Turn left onto this paved road. Drive 2.7 miles (past the F.R. 89 turnoff to Whitetop Mountain) and park at the large parking lot on the left at Elk Garden.

Elevation change: The ride begins at an elevation of 4,500 feet at Elk Garden. There is a slight elevation gain on S.R. 600, but the serious ascent begins on F.R. 89; you will reach an elevation of about 5,000 feet in the first few miles. A final gain is tallied on the switchbacks to the top of the mountain. At the summit of Whitetop Mountain, you will reach a maximum elevation of about 5,500 feet. The total elevation gain is 1,000 feet; total elevation loss is 1,000 feet.

Configuration: Out-and-back

Snow-crusted summit of Whitetop Mountain

This is a moderately difficult ride which begins on a paved secondary road, S.R. 600. This road, which has a relatively easy grade, is flanked by a mixed hardwood forest. A right turn on F.R. 89 will start you on a gradual climb toward the peak of Whitetop Mountain. At an elevation of 5,520 feet, the vegetation found on this mountaintop is more similar to vegetation found in Canada than what is typical of Virginia.

The dirt road to the summit cuts a fairly straightforward path between walls of tall, slender hardwood trees. You will enjoy a brief reprieve from the climb after less than a mile on this road, though the climbing continues with a vengeance about half a mile later.

When you reach the switchbacks in the road (and the 5,000-foot elevation line), you will find that the scenery changes dramatically. Rather than cycling through a heavily forested area, you will find yourself pedaling across an open bald. The vastness is occasionally interrupted by a shock of evergreens permanently bent and contorted by blustery winds, snow, and ice. It is certainly no mystery why the mountain was named Whitetop. On an early-October ride, the bald was already coated with sparkling frost and ice. Local folks say you can expect to find the top of this mountain snow- or ice-covered as late as the month of May. So, even though you may be comfortable down in the valley wearing bicycling shorts and a T-shirt, be prepared.

Near the top of the mountain, the road is littered with rocks and potholes. Though the ride is not technical, these obstructions will require that you pick a line to avoid tweaking a tire and crashing. Panoramic views of Buzzard Rock, Beech Mountain, and other surrounding mountains of Virginia, Tennessee, and North Carolina make the climbing worthwhile.

0.0 From the parking lot at Elk Garden, cycle south on S.R. 600, a paved road.

1.2 Turn right onto F.R. 89, a dirt road. You will continue a gradual climb.

1.9 The grade of the road levels out.

2.5 The road begins climbing again.

3.0 You will pass a parking lot on your right. Continue through the open gate, which is closed during the winter. You will notice a great view of Pond Mountain on the left. The vegetation changes at this point as you enter the bald area.

4.0 Turn left after the parking lot. The road on the right leads up to an FAA navigational complex, which is quite impressive.

4.1 There is a nice view of Buzzard Rock in the corner of the field below. At the top of the mountain, turn around and begin retracing your path. It's downhill from here. Enjoy the descent. You've earned it! Also be cautious of vehicles, as this is a well-traveled road.

8.2 Arrive back at the parking area.

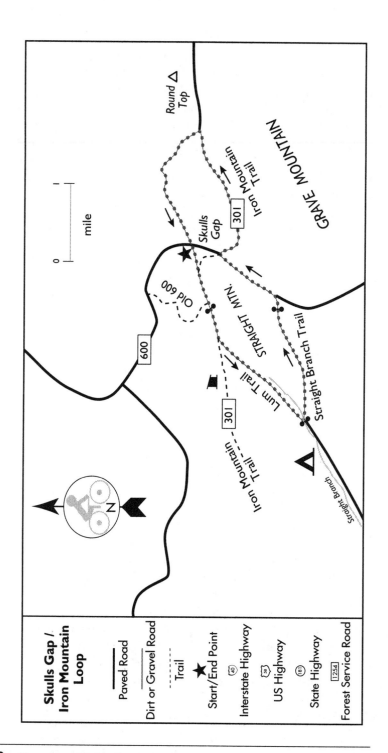

Skulls Gap /
Iron Mountain Loop

Distance: 8.8 miles

Difficulty: Strenuous

Riding Surface: Old-forest road, single-track trail, paved road, dirt road

Maps: 1. Mount Rogers National Recreation Area
2. USGS 7.5 minute quadrangle, Konnarock, Va.
3. USGS 7.5 minute quadrangle, Whitetop Mountain, Va.
4. Mount Rogers National Recreation Area Trail Town Maps, Trail Guide to Beartree/ Damascus, Va., Area

Access: From the intersection of U.S. 58 and Va. 91, take U.S. 58 East. Drive 9.7 miles to the intersection with Va. 603 at Konnarock. U.S. 58 makes a sharp right here. Continue straight on Va. 603. After 2.9 miles, you will pass Weaver Grocery. Continue straight on Va. 600 for 2.2 miles. Part of this route was opened as recently as 1997. The Skulls Gap Picnic Area is on the left. The entrance is marked by a sign. Park and start your ride here. **Note:** If you are using a map drawn prior to 1997, the Skulls Gap Picnic Area will be on the right side of Va. 600.

Elevation change: From the 3,300-foot elevation at the Skulls Gap Picnic Area, the ride begins with a short descent of 160 feet to the Iron Mountain Trail turnoff from "Old 600." The route climbs 600 feet to Lum Trail. There is a 400-foot descent to the end of Lum Trail at Chipmunk

Circle. Straight Branch Trail then climbs 240 feet to a hilltop clearing, before dropping 240 feet to Va. 600. The climb on Va. 600 gains 260 feet. There is a gradual climb of 320 feet for the next 0.6 mile on Iron Mountain Trail. From the Iron Mountain Trail/F.R. 84 intersection, there is a 880-foot drop to the starting point at the Skulls Gap Picnic Area. Total elevation gain is 1,420 feet; total elevation loss is 1,680 feet.

Configuration: Loop

The Skulls Gap area has changed dramatically since the summer of 1997. Va. 600 has been rerouted to cut straight across the mountain and down into the valley below. If you are using a map drawn before 1997, you may be disoriented. The Skulls Gap Picnic Area is now on the west side of Va. 600, not on the east side. "Old 600" was graded and planted with grass, which makes for a very nice trail. A short section of Old 600, which comes out of the Skulls Gap Picnic Area, is now part of the Iron Mountain Trail. The Iron Mountain Trail now starts across from the picnic area. The new section enters the forest and climbs gently up Iron Mountain.

The United States Forest Service coordinated volunteers from all over the United States and the world to relocate the Iron Mountain Trail. It is an inspiration to see the results of their efforts, especially when you consider that it was all built with hand tools. Thank you, volunteers!

A previous re-routing of the Iron Mountain Trail followed F.R. 84. Although that route is no longer the official route, some of the yellow blazes along that stretch still remain.

There are a number of different routes that can be taken for this ride, but a route ending with a nice, long downhill ride seems preferable. Ride it any way you want, but make sure you do try this one. It is destined to become a classic.

After leaving the Skulls Gap Picnic Area and entering the woods for the Iron Mountain Trail, you will encounter a bit of climbing on a nice single-track trail. This is a great way to start your ride.

Rocky creekbeds are frequent in Southwest Virginia.

After turning onto Lum Trail, you will descend for one mile on one of the area's prettiest single tracks. This trail winds alongside the headwaters of Straight Branch Creek—a creek that is anything but straight. The trail has a few tricky creek crossings, including one that has a small rock-ledge dropoff. Watch for hikers as you come into Beartree Recreation Area. This trail is a popular hiking trail for campers staying here.

From the recreation area, Straight Branch Trail takes you toward Va. 600 It's about 0.7 mile from the recreation area to a field where a large sign describes the destruction Hurricane Hugo caused to this area in 1989.

At the junction of Va. 600 and Straight Branch Trail, you will see what one British cyclist described as "one bloody, long slog" up the mountain. It is unavoidable, so just resolve to start turning the cranks to climb to the crest of the mountain.

This section can be especially bothersome during a hot summer day because the new pavement on Va. 600 is black as a butyl tube.

At the crest of the mountain, you will finally get to ride on the new section of the Iron Mountain Trail. This route, which climbs gradually back to F.R. 84, takes you into the cool shade of the forest. Make sure you check out the views as you climb because they are spectacular—especially in the fall. At one point, you will look at the ridge of Grave Mountain. Beyond that ridge is the summit of Whitetop Mountain. If it's clear, you may even be able to see the bald on the end of Whitetop Mountain, which is the second-highest mountain in Virginia (elevation 5,520 feet).

Once you reach F.R. 84, be ready for a fast descent on this dirt road back to where you started at Skulls Gap.

0.0   From the Skulls Gap Picnic Area, turn west onto Va. 600.

0.1   Bear right after going through the pole gate. On the left is a yellow blaze on a tree. Descend on "Old 600."

0.5   Turn left onto Iron Mountain Trail. Go through a metal gate and follow the yellow rectangle blazes. You will begin a steep climb.

0.9   The trail levels out.

1.1   Continue straight when you reach a big meadow. Follow the yellow blazes on the apple trees in the meadow. There is an old log structure on the left at the far edge of the meadow.

1.2   Continue straight as you head back into the woods. You will have a very short climb.

1.3   At the intersection of Iron Mountain and Lum Trails, turn left onto Lum Trail, following the yellow diamond blazes. To the right of Lum Trail is the Straight Branch

Shelter. You will also find directional signs here. This is the starting point for a fun, 1.0-mile descent.

2.3 When you arrive on the paved road at Chipmunk Circle Camping Area, turn left. This camping area is part of Beartree Recreation Area. There are bathrooms on the right.

2.4 Follow the directional signs in the camping area and turn left onto Straight Branch Trail, heading toward Va. 600.

3.1 Continue straight at the clearing marked with a number 37 on a tree. Take time to read the sign, which explains the damage caused by Hurricane Hugo in 1989. From here, you will start to descend.

3.8 Pass through a wooden gate.

3.9 Turn left onto Va. 600 and start the "bloody, long slog" up the paved road ahead.

4.6 At the crest of the hill, turn right at the crosswalk and go through the break in the guardrail. Follow the yellow rectangle blazes into the forest.

4.7 Turn right onto the new route for Iron Mountain Trail.

5.2 On the right is a great view of the ridge of Grave Mountain. Behind that is Whitetop Mountain.

5.3 The new section of the Iron Mountain Trail converges with the old section here. The difference in trail width is evident. Follow the yellow rectangle blazes as you crest the hill and descend.

6.6 Turn left onto F.R. 84, heading toward Va. 600. Enjoy the downhill.

6.8 On the right is a good view of the valley below.

7.5 Continue descending on F.R. 84. The intersection with "Old 84" is past the gate on your right.

8.6 Go straight as you cross Va. 600, heading back into the Skulls Gap Picnic Area.

8.8 Arrive back at the Skulls Gap Picnic Area.

You may have to cross a few fallen trees along the way.

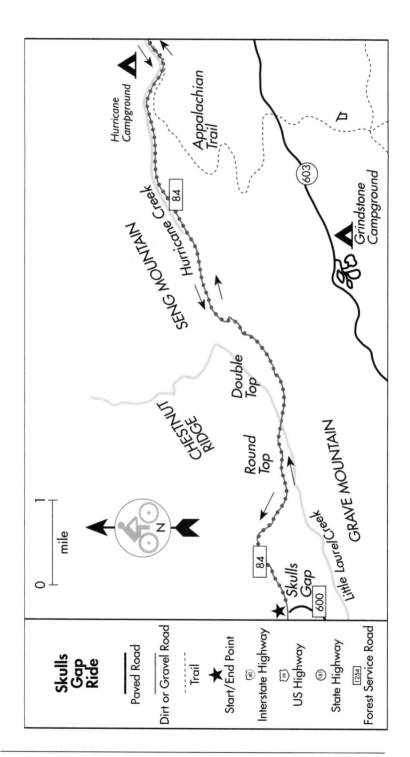

Skulls Gap Ride

Distance: 17.8 miles

Difficulty: Moderately strenuous

Riding Surface: Dirt-and-gravel road

Maps: 1. Mount Rogers National Recreation Area
2. USGS 7.5 minute quadrangle, Whitetop. Va.
3. USGS 7.5 minute quadrangle, Troutdale, Va.
4. Mount Rogers Recreation Area Trail Town Maps, Trail Guide to Beartree/ Damascus, Va., Area

Access: From the intersection of U.S. 58 and Va.91, take U.S. 58 East. Drive 9.7 miles to the intersection with Va. 603 at Konnarock. U.S. 58 makes a sharp right here. Continue straight on Va. 603. After 2.9 miles, you will pass Weaver Grocery. Continue straight on Va. 600 for 2.2 miles. Part of this route was opened as recently as 1997. The Skulls Gap Picnic Area is on the left. The entrance is marked by a sign. Park and start your ride here. **Note:** If you are using a map drawn prior to 1997, the Skulls Gap Picnic Area will be on the right side of Va. 600.

Elevation change: From the 3,500-foot elevation at Skulls Gap, the ride begins with a descent to 3,400 feet before rising back to 3,500 feet. It then rises steadily to a maximum elevation of 4,200 feet near Double Top Mountain. A descent to the minimum elevation of 2,700 feet along Hurricane Creek at the campground follows. You will then turn around and retrace your path to the starting point at the Skulls Gap Picnic Area. The total elevation gain is 2,400 feet; total elevation loss is 2,400 feet.

Configuration: Out-and-back

his is a formidable ride softened only by blessed down hills and pristine wilderness surroundings. The road winds up and down the hills of Iron Mountain as it leaves Skulls Gap in pursuit of Hurricane Gap. High ridge-top sections offer beautiful views of nearby mountains and distant towns nestled in the valley. The scenery varies from gray hardwood trunks adorned with green, leafy tresses in summer to the verdant creekside flora that colors the landscape year-round. It is along these damp banks that glossy-leaved rhododendron bushes mingle with the lacy fringes of hemlock trees. An early-summer ride is certain to make you catch your breath when you round the first bend near Hurricane Creek and are bombarded with the stunning sight and the fragrant scent of pink rhododendron blossoms.

The ride is not technically challenging; the rough and rocky stretches of road that were here previously have been graded and smoothed out. This out-and-back route will lead you to dry ridge lines high in the hills and drop you down beside picturesque mountain creeks. It will give you just about all you could ask for from a physical workout in perhaps the most beautiful natural gym around.

0.0 From the Skulls Gap Picnic Area, turn left, following the new portion of Va. 600.

0.2 Cross the new portion of Va. 600, following F.R. 84.

0.3 The road begins to climb. You will see the creek on the left side of the road.

1.1 The road starts to level out.

1.3 The road starts to descend.

1.4 You will reach a Y-intersection where you will take a sharp right to stay on F.R. 84. There is a gated road on the left, which leads to Old 84 and Jerry's Creek Trail. The metal gate has a sign saying it is closed to all motor vehicles. You will begin a climb just past this intersection.

2.0 On the left, there are good views of the valley below.

2.1 The road starts to descend.

2.3 Iron Mountain Trail comes into the road from the right. This section was closed for two years, just re-opening in late 1997. Iron Mountain Trail will run conjunctively with F.R. 84 for awhile. Continue straight.

3.3 On the right, you will see a clearing with a tree marked with the number 47. Iron Mountain Trail turns back into the forest on the right. Continue straight.

4.3 F.R. 828 intersects with F.R. 84. Continue straight on F.R. 84. You can now follow the orange diamonds marking the Virginia Highlands Horse Trail, which is running conjunctively with F.R. 84 at this point. The road will start to descend.

4.8 Old 84/Rowland Creek Trail intersects from the left. Continue straight.

6.8 Barton Gap Trail enters from the left. Continue straight.

7.5 You will pass an unmarked single-track trail on the left.

8.6 You will pass a dirt road with a wooden gate.

8.9 You will arrive at a stop sign near the entrance to Hurricane Campground. Turn around and begin retracing your path. (**Note:** You can cut this ride in half and eliminate the toughest climb by leaving a vehicle at the campground and setting up a shuttle.)

17.8 Arrive back at Skulls Gap Picnic Area.

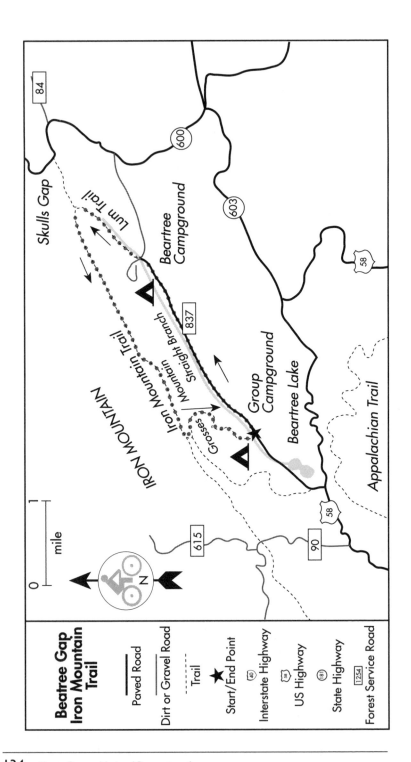

Beatree Gap Iron Mountain Trail

Paved Road

Dirt or Gravel Road

- - - Trail

★ Start/End Point

Interstate Highway

US Highway

State Highway

Forest Service Road

Skulls Gap

Lum Trail

IRON MOUNTAIN

Iron Mountain Trail

Iron Mountain Branch Straight Branch

837

Grosses

Beartree Campground

Group Campground

Beartree Lake

Appalachian Trail

N

mile

0   1

84

600

603

58

58

615

90

Beartree Gap / Iron Mountain Trail Loop

Distance: 10.2 miles

Difficulty: Moderate

Riding surface: Paved road, single-track trail

Maps: 1. Mount Rogers National Recreation Area
2. USGS 7.5 minute quadrangle, Konnarock, Va.
3. Mt. Rogers Recreation Area Trail Town Maps, Trail Guide to Beartree/ Damascus, Va., Area

Access: From the intersection of U.S. 58 and Va. 91, take U.S. 58 East. After 6.8 miles, turn left onto Beartree Gap Road (F.R. 837). Travel 0.2 mile toward Beartree Group Campground and turn right into the fisherman's parking lot near the fee station.

Elevation change: From an elevation of 3,000 feet at the fisherman's parking lot, the ride climbs 300 feet on a paved road to Lum Trail. Continuing on Lum Trail, the route gains another 500 feet, reaching 3,800 feet at the intersection with Iron Mountain Trail. The ride eventually reaches a maximum elevation of 3,950 feet before it drops back to 3,800 feet. On the descent into Shaw Gap, the elevation quickly drops 240 feet. As the trail continues, you drop another 440 feet before reaching the group campground area. Before returning to the starting point, you descend another 125 feet. Total elevation gain is 950 feet; total elevation loss is 950 feet.

Configuration: Loop

A 3-mile climb up the paved Beartree Gap Road provides a perfect warm-up for the real climb awaiting you at Chipmunk Circle camping area. The natural beauty of the forest flanking the road is highlighted by the trickling waters of Straight Branch Creek, located on the north side of the road. You will have a closer view of this pretty mountain stream when you begin cycling the first single-track trail of this loop, Lum Trail.

Once on Lum Trail, you will have a chance to exercise your technical prowess. The trail is strewn with rocks and roots, which will keep you on your toes. Though it begins as a wide single track with plenty of maneuvering room, it squeezes down to a very narrow path which makes for a tight fit for you and your mountain bike. The grade is level at the beginning of the trail but steepens to a strenuous climb on the approach to Iron Mountain Trail. If you are exhausted by the time you reach the Straight Branch Shelter located on the left side of Lum Trail, then you're in trouble, because the real climbing is about to begin.

A left turn onto the yellow-blazed Iron Mountain Trail will

Taking a breather on the Iron Mountain Trail

find you on a narrow trail surrounded by a mature hardwood forest. This trail was formerly part of the Appalachian Trail, which is why it has shelters at various points along its length. Iron Mountain Trail takes you along the rolling ridge of Grosses Mountain. This part of the trail is known for its grassy single track. It also has large rocks embedded in the trail, which can present a distraction to the views from the ridge. It's all rideable, but you need to choose your line carefully. There are some tricky log crossings and large rocks in the middle of the trail that often seem to appear out of nowhere.

Iron Mountain Trail descends to Shaw Gap on a steep section composed of loose rocks. Consideration is being given to relocating this section of trail, but there are no definite plans as of this writing. At Shaw Gap, you will find an intersection of four trails: Iron Mountain, Shaw Gap, Beartree Gap, and Chestnut Ridge Trails.

From this intersection, get ready to experience the thrill of Shaw Gap Trail, a tight, twisting, 1-mile single-track masterpiece. As the trail slices across Grosses Mountain on its way down to the campground, it narrows and becomes very technical. There are some grassy sections that will spit you through tight tunnels of mountain laurel, creating a wildly sensational descent. Then, just before the campground, the trail blows out of the dense forest and lands in an open meadow.

0.0 Starting from the fisherman's parking lot, turn right toward the pay station on Beartree Gap Road.

0.5 Pass through the gate at the pay station. If you are on a bike, you do not have to pay. This gate may be locked in the winter months. Pass Yancey Trail on the left.

1.2 Pass the entrance to the group campground on your left. You will return to this point near the end of the ride.

3.5 Turn left at the cul-de-sac, which is located at the entrance to Chipmunk Circle camping area. Pass Straight Branch Trail on your right.

Wimping out on a technical section of trail

3.6   Turn right onto Lum Trail, which is marked with yellow diamonds. The trailhead is a bit hidden; it is located just behind the restrooms.

3.8   Continue straight on Lum Trail. An unmarked trail turns off to the right.

4.5   This is the last climb on Lum Trail. Stick to it!

4.6   Arrive at Straight Branch Shelter on your left. Continue straight, following the trail marked by the tree with the yellow, diamond-shaped blaze.

4.7 Turn left onto Iron Mountain Trail. Look for the yellow rectangles to follow the well-blazed Iron Mountain Trail. Start a short steep climb here.

5.0 There are good views off both sides of the trail. Looking to the north you can see Little Mountain; to the south, Konnarock. This beautiful, rolling ridge-top ride has three short, steep climbs.

7.6 Descend a rough, rocky section into Shaw Gap. Use caution, as there are ruts where erosion has occurred.

7.8 At the Shaw Gap intersection where four trails meet, turn left, following the trail marked by yellow, square-shaped blazes. Beartree Gap Trail, which turns to the right, is marked with yellow diamonds. (**Note:** This major trail intersection serves as an important navigational point for many rides in this area. The trails are well marked thanks to the United States Forest Service and the Iron Mountain Trail Club.)

8.3 Shaw Gap Trail levels out, but there will be more downhill to come. The rhododendron that surrounds the trail makes for limited sight distance, so use caution.

8.8 There is a clearing on the right. On the left, you look down into the group campground.

8.9 Turn left onto a paved road at the group campground.

9.0 Turn right after leaving the campground area; go through the gate and turn right onto Beartree Gap Road.

10.2 Turn left into the fisherman's parking lot, where you started.

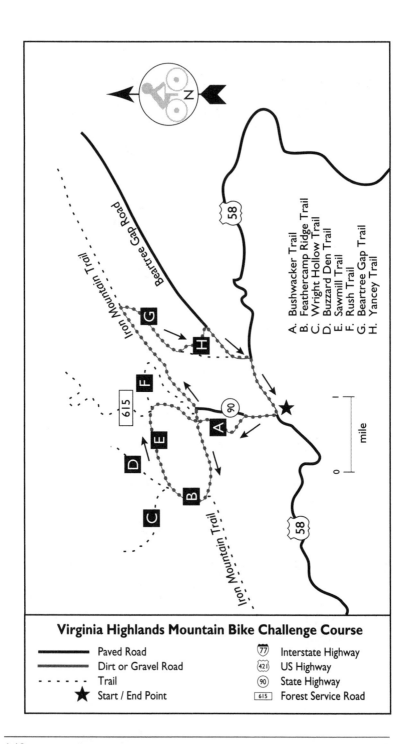

Virginia Highlands Mountain Bike Challenge Course

——— Paved Road	(77) Interstate Highway
▨▨▨▨ Dirt or Gravel Road	(421) US Highway
- - - - - Trail	(90) State Highway
★ Start / End Point	[615] Forest Service Road

A. Bushwacker Trail
B. Feathercamp Ridge Trail
C. Wright Hollow Trail
D. Buzzard Den Trail
E. Sawmill Trail
F. Rush Trail
G. Beartree Gap Trail
H. Yancey Trail

Virginia Highlands Mountain Bike Challenge Course

Distance: 12.8 miles

Difficulty: Moderate to strenuous

Length: 12.8 miles

Riding Surface: Gravel road, grassy double-track trail, and single-track trail

Maps: 1. Mount Rogers National Recreation Area
2. USGS 7.5 minute quadrangle, Konnarock, Va.
3. Mount Rogers National Recreation Area Trail Town Maps, Trail Guide to Beartree/ Damascus, Va., Area

Access: From the intersection of U.S. 58 and Va. 91, take U.S. 58 East. Drive approximately 6 miles to the intersection with F.R. 90. Turn left onto F.R. 90 and park at a pull-off on the right.

Elevation change: The loop begins at an elevation of about 2,900 feet on F.R. 90. It climbs steadily to 3,100 feet at the first turnoff. You will gain another 400 feet on this grassy, double-track section of Bushwacker Trail, reaching a maximum of 3,500 feet. A descent of 140 feet to F.R. 90 follows. On Iron Mountain Trail, you will climb to the tune of 150 feet of elevation, before dropping 100 feet to the Sawmill Trail intersection. You lose another 360 feet on the descent to the F.R. 615 intersection. Then it's a steady climb of 400 feet on F.R. 615 to the F.R. 90/Iron Mountain Trail intersection. In the next 1.4 miles, you gain about 450 feet, cresting the top of the ridge at an elevation of 3,805 feet. Prepare for the descent of 240 feet into Shaw Gap. Then it's on to Beartree Gap Trail. You gain about 50 feet, then drop 540 feet over a 1.7-mile section of the course before reaching Beartree Gap Road. You drop another 40 feet as you return to the starting point. Total elevation gain is 1,650 feet; total elevation loss is 1,420 feet.

Configuration: Loop

The Virginia Highlands Mountain Bike Challenge is a mountain-bike race held in early May of each year. This ride follows the original course that Teddy Helton laid out for the first race in 1993. The Virginia Highlands Mountain Bike Challenge has become a local favorite and has drawn an average of 130 competitors each year for the last five years.

The loop is an invigorating combination of grassy logging roads, narrow single-track trials, and climbing gravel roads. The climbing sections are sandwiched between intermittent downhills, tempering the overall severity of the ride. Some of these downhills are gentle enough to give you a chance to catch your breath. But others don't give you much time to relax. Some of these paths follow tight, technical single-track trails that dangle on the edge of steep ridges. As your wheels tiptoe down the only line possible, you realize that there isn't much margin for error. Others are near-vertical descents that bottom out in streams filled with slippery, moss-covered stones.

The Feathercamp Ridge Trail section of the course was almost "lost" after an ice storm in 1993 felled a large number of trees. The fallen canopy made the trail almost invisible. This natural disaster almost ended the first challenge race, but the hard work and sweat of numerous volunteers from the tri-state area cleared the trail in time for the race.

The winner of the race usually does this course in a little less than one hour, but this course also makes a great day ride for those who are more laid back. The course offers some of the area's premier single-track biking.

Pedaling up the gravel road of F.R. 615

0.0 From the intersection of F.R. 90 and U.S. 58, proceed up F.R. 90.

0.5 Turn left and pass through a metal gate onto Bushwacker Trail. The suggested line actually travels between two large rocks almost parallel to the right side of the gate. There is a trail sign indicating Bushwacker Trail, which is blazed with yellow diamonds. You will begin a climb on this grassy double track.

1.0 To the right of the grassy double track, you will see a large rock pile and a log at the entrance to a single-track trail on the right. Turn onto this single track. About 50 feet from the beginning of this single track, you will see a yellow diamond blaze on a tree. At this point, you will need to dismount and carry your bike up the very short hill. If you start to descend on the grassy double track, you have missed the turn.

Rock walls line the trail, creating a scenic mountain-bike ride.

1.1 The trail turns right and crosses the creek. It ascends, levels out, then starts to descend.

1.2 The trail levels out as you crest the hill.

1.5 At the intersection of Iron Mountain and Bushwacker Trails, continue straight on Bushwacker Trail. There is a directional trail sign here and Sandy Flats Shelter will be on the left.

1.7 Bushwacker Trail ends at the gravel F.R. 90 and F.R. 615. Bear left around the upper right gate. The lower left gate is marked by blue blazes, which indicate the hiker-only Feathercamp Trail.

1.8 Turn left off the grassy double-track F.R. 90 onto Iron Mountain Trail. Look for yellow rectangle blazes.

1.9 The hiker-only section of Iron Mountain Trail intersects from the left; continue straight. There is a double yellow blaze on a post at this directional trail sign. Start a gradual, technical climb.

2.4 Crest the ridge and get ready for some descending, narrow single track. If it's the right time of year, this spot is covered with blueberries.

2.7 At the T-intersection, you will see a directional sign that says "Damascus 6." There will also be a yellow rectangle blaze on a big oak tree to the left. Feathercamp Ridge Trail, which goes to the right, is blazed with yellow triangles. Turn right onto Feathercamp Ridge Trail. In the next 0.6 mile, you will descend a steep slope, ride over rubber water bars, cross a creek, travel down a new log ramp, and pedal over a log French drain.

3.5 Bear to the right immediately after crossing the log French drain. Look for the yellow diamond blaze and directional sign for Sawmill Trail. Do not take Wright Hollow Trail. Go about 50 yards and take a sharp left turn onto Sawmill Trail. Look for the yellow diamond blaze on the tree.

3.7 You will pass the intersection with Buzzard Den Ridge Trail. Bear right downhill, following the yellow diamond blazes. Your ride on this trail will be a descent with only a few short climbs. Enjoy the long downhill and the views.

4.9 As you enter a wildlife clearing with the number 15

painted on the trees, bear right. You will begin a long descent.

5.3 Go around the gate and turn right onto F.R. 615.

6.5 At the intersection of F.R. 615 and F.R. 90, turn left onto the gravel F. R. 90.

7.0 At the crest of the hill, look for the yellow rectangle blazes on the tree near the trailhead. Turn left onto Iron Mountain Trail. Proceed about 50 yards before turning right. You will still be following the yellow rectangle blazes marking the Iron Mountain Trail.

7.1 You will climb a steep hill, which has rubber-belt water bars. The cruise along the spine of Iron Mountain has some nice rolling climbs and descents. This is a typical section of Iron Mountain Trail with large embedded rocks and grassy single track.

8.5 Descend a steep hill that has rubber-belt water bars and log check-dams installed on it. At the bottom of the hill is Shaw Gap, a major intersection for many of the trails around Beartree Recreation Area.

8.7 Turn right onto Beartree Gap Trail, marked by yellow diamond blazes. Beartree Gap Trail is also blazed with old purple blazes, but they are very faint.

10.4 Look for the yellow squares that mark Yancey Trail. Turn left onto Yancey Trail, heading on a long downhill section. You follow Yancey Trail to the Beartree pay station. The trail will turn to gravel near the end.

11.4 Turn right at the pay station and ride down the paved Beartree Gap Road to Va. 58.

12.0 Turn right onto Va. 58 and descend to the intersection with F.R. 90.

12.8 Arrive back at the pullover area where you started.

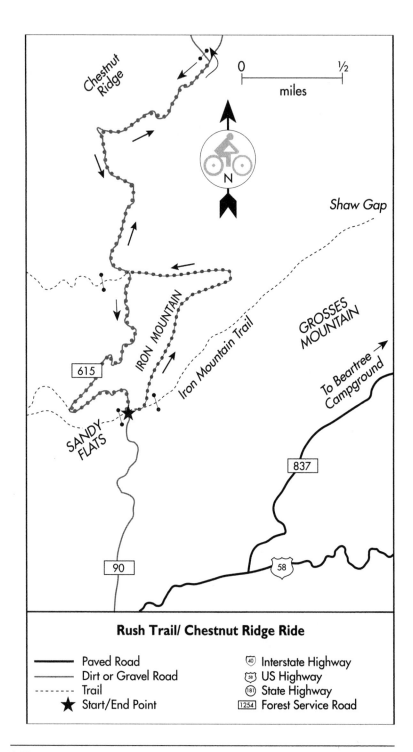

Chestnut Ridge

0   ½

miles

N

Shaw Gap

IRON MOUNTAIN

Iron Mountain Trail

GROSSES MOUNTAIN

To Beartree Campground

615

SANDY FLATS

837

90

58

Rush Trail/ Chestnut Ridge Ride

▬▬▬ Paved Road	ⓐ Interstate Highway
▬▬▬ Dirt or Gravel Road	ⓤ US Highway
- - - - Trail	ⓢ State Highway
★ Start/End Point	1254 Forest Service Road

Rush Trail /
Chestnut Ridge Ride

Distance: 7.2 miles

Difficulty: Moderate

Riding Surface: Single-track trail, gravel forest road

Maps: 1. Mount Rogers National Recreation Area
2. USGS 7.5 minute quadrangle, Konnarock, Va.
3. Mount Rogers National Recreation Area Trail Town Maps, Trail Guide to Beartree/ Damascus, Va., Area

Access: From the intersection of U.S. 58 and Va. 91, take U.S. 58 East. Drive approximately 6 miles to the intersection of F.R. 90. Turn left onto F.R. 90 and drive 1.4 miles to a small, unpaved parking area at the top of the hill.

Elevation change: The ride begins at an elevation of 3,400 feet. On Rush Trail, the elevation drops 400 feet to approximately 3,000 feet. On F.R. 615, you drop to 2,700 feet when you reach the gate near the end of Chestnut Ridge. The climb back up is a fairly gentle and steady gain of 700 feet. Total elevation gain is 700 feet; total elevation loss is 700 feet.

Configuration: Semi-loop

T his ride starts by taking you down Rush Trail, a beautiful 1.8-mile single track that descends along the side of the mountain and winds its way alongside Rush Creek. This ride is particularly exhilarating early in the morning, when the forest is just coming alive and the air is crisp. Savor this early section, as you will have a fair amount of climbing toward the end of the ride.

From the single track, the route travels on a narrow, gently descending road that ultimately passes along the southern border of Chestnut Ridge. Rather than bursting through the woods in a straight-line shot, the road carves a meandering path through incredibly beautiful forest. These dense woods are filled with typical Appalachian flora: hemlock, pine, rhododendron, mixed hardwoods, and, at the higher elevations, mountain laurel. Because of this mix of conifers and deciduous trees, you can expect to be enveloped by a verdant forest all seasons of the year.

Though most of this route is technically unchallenging, there are rough sections along the way that will have you weaving from one side of the road to the other in order to pedal the path of least resistance. Other sections, smooth and groomed, offer a respite where you can examine the forest carefully, especially the old-growth section of hemlocks. These huge trees have a majestic aura all their own. You will probably feel humble as you pass these centuries-old wonders.

Note: These forest roads are lightly traveled except during deer season. In November, you are advised to use caution!

0.0   Proceed east, following the yellow rectangle blazes that indicate Iron Mountain Trail. Do not follow F.R. 90. You will only travel about 100 feet before you see a grassy double-track trail that branches to the left. Turn left and follow the yellow square blazes onto Rush Trail.

0.4   On the left side of the trail, there is a large, old-growth hemlock tree. Continue descending down this trail.

1.2 Cross Rush Creek. The trail becomes wet and rocky. Continue descending.

1.8 At the intersection of F.R. 615 and Rush Trail, turn right onto F.R. 615 and begin a short climb.

2.2 The rolling terrain of F.R. 615 becomes rocky. When the leaves are off the trees, there are some good views on the left.

3.1 The road begins to descend.

3.6 Turn around here and retrace your route on F.R. 615.

4.1 The road levels out.

4.5 Start descending.

5.5 At the intersection with Rush Trail, continue straight on F.R. 615. (**Note:** If you want to retrace your route on Rush Trail, the return trip offers a fun and challenging climb.)

5.6 At the Sawmill Trail intersection, you will pass a metal gate on the right. Continue straight on F.R. 615. It's climbing time again!

6.4 There is a beautiful stand of old-growth forest on your right. Note the large hemlock trees next to the road.

6.7 F.R. 615 ends at the intersection with F.R. 90. Turn left onto F.R. 90 and climb the hill.

7.2 You are back where you started.

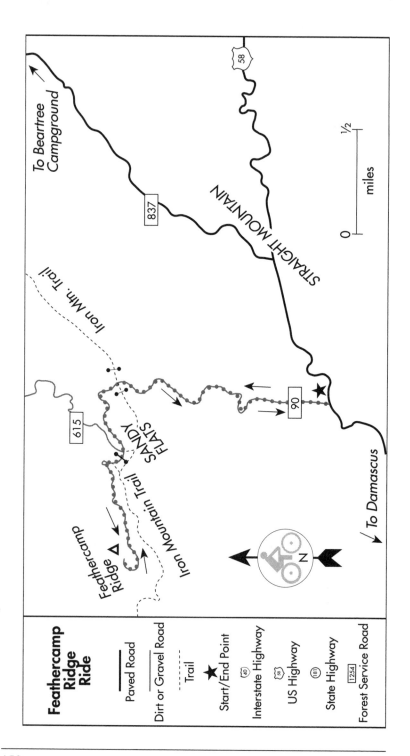

Feathercamp Ridge Ride

Paved Road

Dirt or Gravel Road

Trail

★ Start/End Point

🛣40 Interstate Highway

〰58 US Highway

⑱ State Highway

1254 Forest Service Road

Feathercamp Ridge Ride

Distance: 5.4 miles

Difficulty: Moderate

Riding Surface: Dirt road, grassy double-track trail

Maps: 1. Mount Rogers National Recreation Area
2. USGS 7.5 minute quadrangle, Konnarock, Va.
3. Mount Rogers National Recreation Area Trail Town Maps, Trail Guide to Beartree/ Damascus, Va., Area

Access: From the intersection of U.S. 58 and Va. 91, take U.S. 58 East. Drive approximately 6 miles to the intersection with F.R. 90. Turn left onto F.R. 90 and park at any nearby pull-off.

Elevation change: The ride begins at an elevation of 2,800 feet and quickly climbs to 3,400 feet in the first mile. The elevation remains constant through Sandy Flats. The climbing resumes on the stretch of grassy double track leading up to the former site of the Feathercamp Lookout Tower. The maximum elevation is 3,750 feet. After climbing about 80 feet, it's all downhill to the starting point. The total elevation gain is 950 feet; total elevation loss is 950 feet.

Configuration: Out-and-back

This is an ideal ride if you are short on daylight and want to get in a good workout before the sun drops from the sky and disappears in the dark shadows of the mountains. It is also a great wet-weather ride, as it provides an alternative to riding the more fragile single tracks under muddy conditions.

For most of the route, you follow a hard-packed-dirt forest-service road as it slices across Iron Mountain and climbs to the top of Feathercamp Ridge. F.R. 90 is now gated at its intersection with F.R. 615. This section was graded, drainage dips were added, and grass was planted on the old roadbed. Be forewarned: this grassy section has many loose rocks that can surprise you coming downhill.

Loggers have cleared some sections of forest along the road, creating outstanding views of Whitetop Mountain, Pond Mountain, and Mount Rogers, this area's namesake and the highest mountain in Virginia. From this vantage, the flat, bald summit of Whitetop Mountain appears to look higher than the hogback shape of Mount Rogers, but in fact, Mount Rogers is king at 5,729 feet, while Whitetop Mountain comes in at 5,520 feet. There are more views of other mountains as you grind to the top of Feathercamp Ridge, but you may not be too interested in scenery by this point in the ride.

Gorgeous, natural scenery highlights this dirt road.

The trip back is a madman descent, with some sections rough and technical, some smooth and sweet. The road swings around tight turns that will have you kicking up dirt and sticks along the shoulders and rubbing elbows with the dense rhododendron thickets. Where the road drops into shady mountain gaps, you'll find that the temperature drops almost as quickly as the elevation.

0.0 Begin cycling at the pull-off on F.R. 90.

0.6 As you continue your climb on F.R. 90, there is a good view of Whitetop and Pond Mountains. Pond Mountain is to the left of Whitetop. Bushwacker Trail turns to the left through the gate. (**Note:** For an alternative route to the intersection of F.R. 90 and F.R. 615, you can follow Bushwacker Trail.)

1.0 A gated logging road forks off to the right; continue straight.

1.4 You will arrive at a small pullover. Iron Mountain Trail crosses F.R. 90 at this point.

1.8 At the intersection of F.R. 90 and F.R. 615, proceed through the upper right gate to stay on F.R. 90. On the left is the gated Feathercamp Trail, marked by blue blazes that indicate a trail for hikers only. Here F.R. 90 turns into a grassy double-track trail.

1.9 Iron Mountain Trail turns off to the left. Continue on the grassy double track as you round a right-hand curve.

2.0 Continue around a left-hand curve. Sawmill Trail is straight ahead through the gate.

2.3 There is a great view on the left. In the distance you may be able to see Pond Mountain. Notice the outline

It's a long walk back if you don't know how to perform basic repairs on the trail.

of a house on the ridge. The state boundaries of Virginia, Tennessee, and North Carolina meet in a corner just below this house.

2.5 To the left, there is a great view of Whitetop Mountain and Mount Rogers. Mount Rogers is to the left and behind Whitetop Mountain. The bald on Whitetop Mountain is usually clearly evident.

2.6 Proceed straight on the trail; a cutoff turns off to the right.

2.7 You will arrive at the former site of the Feathercamp Lookout Tower. The old fire tower and its rock stairs are on the left. On the level piece of ground above these steps are the old cement footers that once supported the tower. Enjoy the view before turning around to retrace the route to your starting point.

5.4 Arrive back at the starting point.

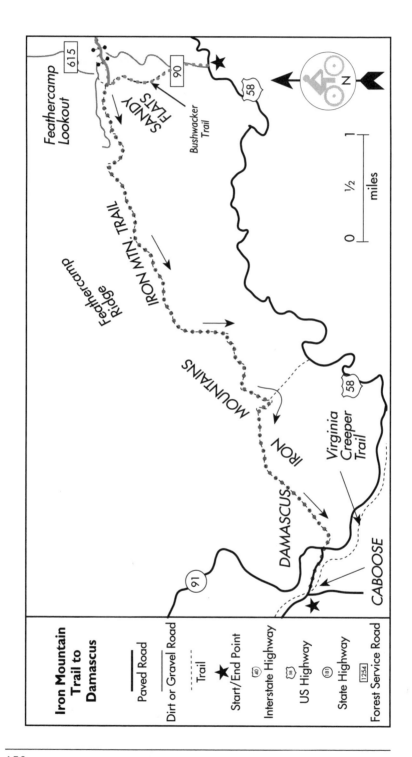

Iron Mountain Trail to Damascus

Paved Road

Dirt or Gravel Road

Trail

★ Start/End Point

40 Interstate Highway

58 US Highway

58 State Highway

1254 Forest Service Road

Feathercamp Lookout

615

90

Bushwacker Trail

SANDY FLATS

58

N

Feathercamp Ridge

IRON MTN. TRAIL

IRON MOUNTAINS

Virginia Creeper Trail

58

DAMASCUS

91

CABOOSE

0   ½   1

miles

Iron Mountain Trail to Damascus

Distance: 8.3 miles

Difficulty: Moderate

Riding Surface: Gravel road, grassy double-track trail, single-track trail

Maps: 1. Mount Rogers National Recreation Area
2. USGS 7.5 minute quadrangle, Konnarock, Va.
3. USGS 7.5 minute quadrangle, Damascus, Va.
4. Mount Rogers National Recreation Area Trail Town Maps, Trail Guide to Beartree/ Damascus, Va., Area

Access: It is recommended that you park one car in Damascus at the town park and take a second car to the pullover on F.R. 90 where the ride begins. If you need to hire a shuttle service in Damascus, see the recommended services described in the chapter, "Virginia Creeper Trail: Whitetop Gap to Damascus."

To reach the pullover on F.R. 90 from the intersection of U.S. 58 and Va. 91, take U.S. 58 East. Drive approximately 6 miles to the intersection with F.R. 90. Turn left onto F.R. 90 and park at any nearby pull-off.

Elevation change: The ride begins at an elevation of 2,900 feet at the F.R. 90 pull-off. It's then a steady 100-foot climb to the first turnoff. The route reaches a maximum elevation of 3,500 feet as you travel on the grassy double-track section of Bushwacker Trail. You descend 140 feet before returning to F.R. 90. You will climb another 150 feet on

Iron Mountain Trail before the trail remains constant for about a mile. This is followed by a steady descent to 2,900 feet, before a final drop to 1,950 feet in Damascus. Total elevation gain is 750 feet; total elevation loss is 1,550 feet.

Configuration: One-way

It's a tight fit, but that just makes it more fun!

Iron Mountain Trail to Damascus is the classic ride for those bikers who want a trail ride that "has it all." You begin with a nice one-mile climb that warms you up for a long downhill that has technical sections to test your bike-handling abilities. The ride along the spine of Iron Mountain has some great views, especially when the leaves are turning in the fall. The descent on the former Appalachian Trail through Mock Holler will test your trail-riding skills if you choose to attempt all the creek crossings without dismounting because each gets progressively more rocky and difficult. Don't let the short distance deceive you; this is a workout.

The first mile follows a gravel forest road before switching to the grassy double-track Bushwacker Trail. You then have to make a short hike-a-bike up the side of a hill to reach the single-track trail. At this point, keep in mind that the worst of the climbing is behind you.

You will pass the Sandy Flats Shelter, which was repaired by the local Iron Mountain Trail Club after it was vandalized in 1996. For most of the rest of the ride to Damascus, you will ride along the ridge of Iron Mountain. The last 2 miles drop through Mock Hollow (or as the locals say, Mock Holler) following the old Appalachian Trail, a rocky, steep double track. The ride winds through five creek crossings before reaching the "holler." Here you may be greeted by some neighborhood dogs. Turn right onto Va. 58, which takes you to the east end of Damascus and back to the town park.

0.0   Begin cycling at the pull-off on F.R. 90. Continue your climb on F.R. 90.

0.5   Turn left and pass through a metal gate onto Bushwacker Trail. The suggested line actually travels between two large rocks almost parallel to right side of the gate. There is a trail sign indicating Bushwacker Trail, which is marked with yellow diamonds. There is a good view of Whitetop and Pond Mountains. Pond Mountain is to the left of Whitetop. You will begin a climb on this grassy double track.

1.0   To the right of the grassy double track, you will see a large rockpile and a log at the entrance to a single-track trail on the right. Turn onto this single track. About 50 feet from the beginning of this single track, you will see a yellow diamond blaze on a tree. At this point, you will need to dismount and carry your bike up the very short hill. If you start to descend on the grassy double track, you have missed the turn.

1.2   The trail levels out as you crest the hill.

1.5   At the intersection of Iron Mountain and Bushwacker

Despite being high in the hills, there are still some level spots on the trails in Mount Rogers National Recreation Area.

Trails, continue straight on Bushwacker Trail. There is a directional trail sign here and Sandy Flats Shelter will be on the left.

1.7 Bushwacker Trail ends at the gravel F.R. 90 and F.R. 615. Bear left around the upper right gate. The lower left gate is marked by blue blazes, which indicate the hiker-only Feathercamp Trail.

1.8 Turn left off the grassy double-track F.R. 90 onto Iron Mountain Trail. Look for yellow rectangle blazes.

1.9 The hiker-only section of Iron Mountain Trail intersects from the left; continue straight. There is a double yellow blaze on a post at this directional trail sign. Start a gradual, technical climb.

2.4 Crest the ridge and get ready for some descending narrow single track. If it's the right time of year, this spot is covered with blueberries.

2.7 Turn left at this T-intersection. Follow the directional sign that says "Damascus 6." There will also be a yellow rectangle blaze on a big oak tree to the left. Feathercamp Ridge Trail, which goes to the right, is part of the Virginia Highlands Mountain Bike Challenge Course described in another chapter.

4.7 The trail intersects with a grassy road that was cut for logging activity that never materialized. Turn left, following the yellow rectangle blazes.

4.9 On the left, you will pass Beach Grove Trail, which is blazed with yellow diamonds.

5.0 When you see the double yellow rectangle blazes, turn left heading back into the forest. If you start to ascend the hill on the grassy road, you missed the turn.

5.1 You will navigate through two switchbacks as you climb a short hill.

6.0 At the intersection, turn right, following the yellow arrow. This trail was formerly part of the Appalachian Trail. The road straight ahead goes to the top of "The Cuckoo," which is a 3,000-foot knob overlooking Damascus. You are now starting two miles of loose-rocky downhill. The first mile is the steepest, so pay attention.

7.0 You will cross the first of five small creeks, which follow in quick succession. Each one gets progressively more technical.

7.5 Iron Mountain Trail ends as you pass through a pole gate. Continue straight on this dirt road.

7.8 Turn right onto Va. 58, following it back to Damascus Town Park.

8.3 Arrive back at the red caboose in Damascus Town Park.

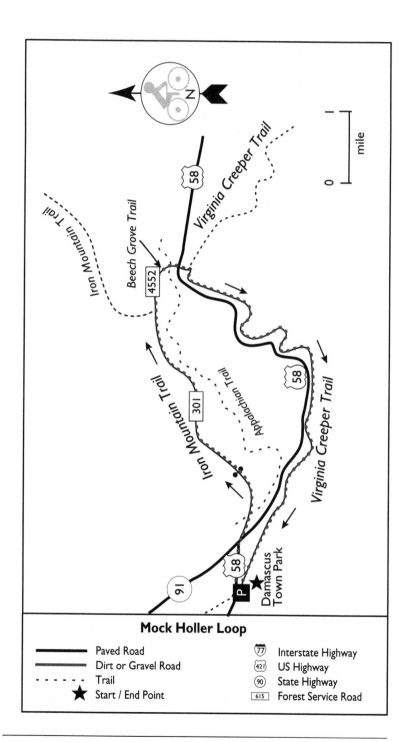

Mock Holler Loop

———	Paved Road	🛣	Interstate Highway
▬▬▬	Dirt or Gravel Road	421	US Highway
- - - - -	Trail	90	State Highway
★	Start / End Point	615	Forest Service Road

Mock Holler Loop

Distance: 9.3 miles

Difficulty: Strenuous and technical

Riding Surface: Old service road, single-track trail, rail trail

Maps: 1. Mount Rogers National Recreation Area
2. USGS 7.5 minute quadrangle, Konnarock, Va.
3. USGS 7.5 minute quadrangle, Damascus, Va.
4. Mount Rogers National Recreation Area Trail Town Maps, Trail Guide to Beartree/ Damascus, Va., Area

Access: The ride starts at Damascus Town Park. To reach the park, you can take Exit 19 from Interstate 81 and follow U. S. 58 East for 12 miles or take U.S. 58 West from the intersection of U.S. 58 and Va. 91. and drive through the town of Damascus for 1.5 miles. From either direction, you look for the red caboose at the Virginia Creeper trailhead. Park in the parking area.

Note: U.S. 58 makes several turns through Damascus; just follow the highway signs and make the appropriate turns.

Elevation change: Mock Holler Loop begins in Damascus at about 1,900 feet. The 2.5-mile climb through Mock Holler to the top of Iron Mountain gains 1,000 feet. The trail then descends 400 feet to the start of Beech Grove Trail. Over the next mile, you descend over 500 feet to the end of Beech Grove Trail. Here you begin the Virginia

Creeper Trail, which is relatively level all the way back to Damascus Town Park. Total elevation gain is 1,000 feet; total elevation loss is 900 feet.

Configuration: Loop

This is an exciting and challenging ride that can test your physical stamina, mental fortitude, and technical ability. Climbing Mock "Holler," which is the colloquialism for Mock Hollow, is one of the rites of passage for the local hammerhead population. You will gain instant respect with this crowd if you can get the two-mile climb through the holler on your resume. To pass the test, you have to ride the "rock garden" at the end of Beech Grove Trail. Be thankful for the work done by United States Forest Service volunteers who have rerouted the trail away from the streambed and built rock water bars. Some local riders were worried that the changes would "sanitize" this section, but it is as technical a challenge as ever. Plenty of locals have left their skin in the rock garden or participated in an endo on this stretch of trail. One guide once said "focus on the negative space between the rocks and flow like water, becoming one with your bike." It takes a great deal of concentration to ride like that, but it works.

After grappling with the rock garden, your reward comes when you can enjoy the ride down to the Virginia Creeper Trail and back to Damascus Town Park.

Note: If you want to turn this ride into a "killer loop," turn left at the intersection with the Virginia Creeper Trail and ride the Taylors Valley Loop, which is described in another chapter. It makes a great day-long ride!

0.0   From the red caboose at Damascus Town Park, proceed toward Whitetop Gap on the Virginia Creeper Trail.

0.1   Cross Shady Avenue, staying on the Virginia Creeper Trail.

A single track in the Mount Rogers National Recreation Area

0.5 Stop at the paved crossing at Orchard Hill Road. Turn left onto U.S. 58. You will pass Dot's Restaurant and the mini-mart on the right.

0.7 Turn right onto East Fourth Street. You are now heading into Mock Holler.

0.8 You are now on a rocky road; bear right at the fork.

1.0 Bear right, go through the pole gate, and follow the yellow rectangle blazes, which designate Iron Mountain Trail. Prepare to cross some small rocky creeks.

1.8 Continue straight. This is where the real climbing begins.

2.5 Turn left, following the yellow rectangle blazes. The climbing is almost over.

2.6 The trail levels out at this point. Ride along this ridge for a short distance before you start a nice descent.

3.5 Still descending, you will come to 2 switchbacks in a grove of hemlock trees.

3.6 Turn right when you intersect with a logging road. Follow this logging road about 100 yards and then turn right onto the yellow-diamond-blazed Beech Grove Trail. Prepare to descend. **Note:** if you start to climb on the logging road, you've missed Beech Grove Trail.

3.8 You will follow a switchback to the right.

3.9 You will come to a very rocky switchback. Be careful! The line runs to the far upper right.

4.0 You will now enter the "rock garden." Choose your line carefully.

4.4 The Appalachian Trail intersects with Beech Grove Trail. Bear left. Do not get on the white-blazed trail. You have survived the rock garden, and the trail gets smoother.

4.6 As you cross U.S. 58, look to the right where you will see the sign for the Virginia Creeper Trail. Turn left and travel through the Straight Branch parking lot.

4.7 Turn right onto the Virginia Creeper Trail, heading toward Damascus. If you want to do the "killer loop," turn left to ride the Taylors Valley Loop.

5.7   There is a beautiful waterfall on right.

7.9   Cross the U.S. 58/ Va. 91 intersection. This is a heavily traveled intersection, so use caution.

9.3   Arrive back at the red caboose at Damascus Town Park.

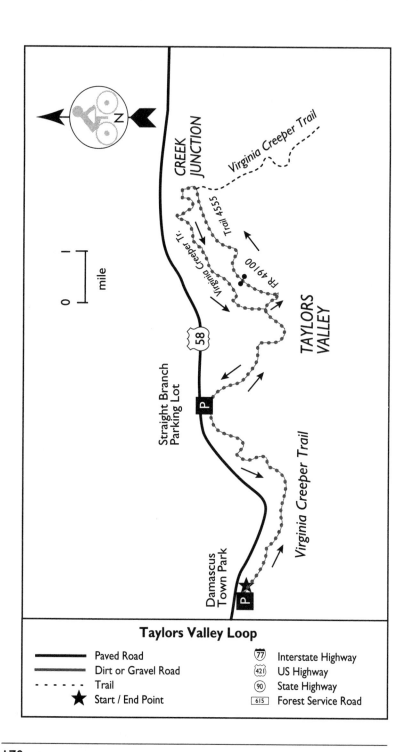

Taylors Valley Loop

——— Paved Road	🛣 77 Interstate Highway
▓▓▓▓ Dirt or Gravel Road	421 US Highway
- - - - - Trail	90 State Highway
★ Start / End Point	615 Forest Service Road

Taylors Valley Loop

Distance: 22.2 miles

Difficulty: Moderate

Riding Surface: Rail trail, gravel road, grassy double-track trail, single-track trail

Maps: 1. Mount Rogers National Recreation Area
        2. USGS 7.5 minute quadrangle, Konnarock, Va.
        3. USGS 7.5 minute quadrangle, Damascus, Va.
        4. Mount Rogers National Recreation Area Trail
           Town Maps, Trail Guide to Beartree/ Damascus,
           Va., Area

Safety Note: You have to cross two creeks at Creek Junction, so check the water level in the stream at Damascus Town Park before you start this ride. Skip this ride if the water is high. You will also get your feet wet, so this ride is best done on a warm, sunny day.

Access: The ride starts at Damascus Town Park. To reach the park, you can take Exit 19 from Interstate 81 and follow U. S. 58 East for 12 miles or take U.S. 58 West from the intersection of U.S. 58 and Va. 91. and drive through the town of Damascus for 1.5 miles. From either direction, you look for the red caboose at the Virginia Creeper trailhead. Park in the parking area.

    Note: U.S. 58 makes several turns through Damascus; just follow the highway signs and make the appropriate turns.

Elevation change: The starting point on the Virginia

Creeper Trail at Damascus Town Park has an elevation of 1,930 feet. The gradual 7.5-mile climb to Taylors Valley has a total elevation gain of 510 feet. The 1.3-mile climb on F.R. 49100/ Taylors Valley Trail gains 600 feet. You then drop 360 feet to Creek Junction. Next comes the Virginia Creeper Trail to Damascus for another descent of 750 feet. Total elevation gain is 1,110 feet; total elevation loss is 1,110 feet.

Configuration: Loop

This loop is long enough for a good workout, technical enough to be a challenge, and beautiful enough to satisfy the nature lover in all of us. One early-autumn trip along this route showed me how abundant the wildlife really is in this area. As I crested a hill on F.R. 49100, I encountered a deer. She was facing away from me, grazing on the grassy trail. She was so oblivious to my presence as I silently approached that I had time to get my camera out, remount my bike, and move even closer to her. When she finally realized something was different, she looked at me, trying to figure out what type of beast I was. She then dashed into the forest, joined by a companion who was just off the trail.

Further down the trail, I watched the fattest groundhog I have ever seen waddle away from the trailside, where he had been eating as if he were taking his last meal before a long winter nap.

As I proceeded back down the Virginia Creeper Trail, a blue heron paced me for half a mile before ducking into the creekbed for a restful drink.

As I approached Taylors Valley, I had just emerged into a sunny patch on the trail when a pair of grouse buzzed right over my head, coming toward me out of the setting sun like two fighter jets strategically waiting for the right moment to launch their surprise attack.

As I approached the Straight Branch parking lot, a turkey hen crossed the trail in front of me and casually meandered

into the forest as I watched her go about her business. It's days like this that remind me that the trails are alive.

This ride begins with a pleasant 7.5-mile ride up the Virginia Creeper Trail's gradual slope to Taylors Valley. At Taylors Valley, you will climb a gravel road to a gate at the top of the ridge. The trail then proceeds on a grassy, rolling double track.

The trail turns into a single track as it descends quickly to Creek Junction. Here you will find an impressive view under one of the highest trestles on the Creeper Trail. Prepare to get your feet wet here because you'll have to cross two creeks at this junction. You'll have plenty of time to dry off as you head for Damascus. The last 11 miles are all downhill on the Virginia Creeper Trail.

0.0 From the red caboose at Damascus Town Park, proceed toward Whitetop Gap on the Virginia Creeper Trail.

0.1 Cross Shady Avenue, staying on the Virginia Creeper Trail.

0.5 Cross the hardtop road and continue on the Virginia Creeper Trail. You will see white blazes along this section because the Appalachian Trail shares the trail corridor.

0.9 The Appalachian Trail leaves the Virginia Creeper Trail, heading up the wooden steps across the road to Iron Mountain. Continue straight.

1.3 Cross the U.S. 58/Va. 91 intersection and bear left toward the sign for the Virginia Creeper Trail. Use caution; the traffic is hazardous!

3.6 There is a beautiful waterfall on the left.

Grassy double track on Taylors Valley Trail

4.6 Pass Straight Branch parking lot on your left. Portable toilets, a donation tube, and a map of the entire Mount Rogers National Recreation Area are all located here.

6.7 Pass through the gate and enter Taylors Valley. There are some picnic tables and drink vending machines located here. This is a good place to stop and stretch your legs before the climb ahead. The Virginia Creeper Trail crosses the paved road and continues straight ahead.

7.0 Cross a trestle. Make sure you shut the gate.

7.3 Pass through a private yard.

7.4 Cross the road, following the Virginia Creeper Trail, which is the lower road.

7.5 Turn right onto F.R. 49100 and follow the gravel road. Do not follow the Virginia Creeper Trail, which heads back into the national forest on the left.

7.8 Bear left on the gravel road.

8.3 As the road levels out at the top of the ridge, bear right.

8.4 Go around the right side of the gate. Descend a rolling, grassy double track. Wildflowers are abundant on this section during the spring and summer.

8.8 Start the last of the big climbs. Watch for wildlife as you crest the hill and start to descend a 0.2-mile-long grassy section. There are some really fun "whoop-te-dos" in the trail!

9.6 Bear right. There is a good view of Iron Mountain to the left.

10.1 Stay to the right as you enter the forest at the crest of the hill.

10.4 Bear right as you emerge from the forest into a clearing marked with the number 14 painted on the trees. Pay attention here! On the right, you will see a grove of 5 big maple trees. The remains of an old homestead are to the left of these trees. One of the trees on the right has a faded blue blaze on it. Just before this tree, you turn right and go through a patch of weeds. There are remains of an old log barn on the right. After going about 50 feet through the weeds, you will come out on a descending single track.

10.7 A faded blue blaze is on the tree to the right. The trail is bounded by rhododendron along this stretch.

10.8 The trail makes a sharp right at a switchback; hit the brakes and continue down the trail.

10.9 Cross to the other side of Green Cove Creek. Proceed to the Creek Junction trestle, which is marked by a blue blaze. Go left toward the concrete pillar, following the trestle. When you reach the pillar, turn right and go under the trestle. The trail is not well defined here, so take your pick on where you want to get wet. Cross to the other side of the second creek, Whitetop Laurel Creek, to reach the road.

10.1 Turn left onto the gravel Creek Junction Road.

11.1 Creek Junction is on your left. Green Cove Creek merges into Whitetop Laurel Creek at this point.

11.5 At the Creek Junction parking lot, turn onto the Virginia Creeper Trail, heading toward Taylors Valley. The Appalachian Trail shares the trail corridor once again.

11.7 The Appalachian Trail turns off to the right. Don't forget; it's for hikers only!

12.8 Notice the downed trees on the right. They are sure signs of beaver activity.

13.8 The two big boulders on the left offer a nice spot for sunning or lunching.

14.5 Cross trestle #28 and enter the Taylors Valley section where you turned off F.R. 49100 earlier. Retrace your path on the Virginia Creeper Trail to Damascus Town Park.

22.2 Arrive at the red caboose in Damascus Town Park.

Southwest Virginia

Rail Trails

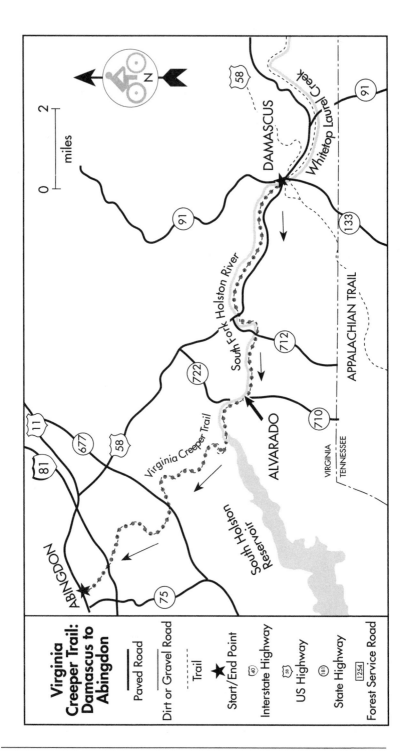

Virginia Creeper Trail: Damascus to Abingdon

Paved Road

Dirt or Gravel Road

Trail

★ Start/End Point

40 Interstate Highway

58 US Highway

81 State Highway

1254 Forest Service Road

DAMASCUS

ALVARADO

ABINGDON

Virginia Creeper Trail

South Fork Holston River

South Holston Reservoir

Whitetop Laurel Creek

APPALACHIAN TRAIL

VIRGINIA
TENNESSEE

N

2

0

miles

58

91

91

133

712

722

710

677

58

11

81

75

Virginia Creeper Trail: Damascus to Abingdon

Distance: 16 miles

Difficulty: Easy

Riding Surface: Rail trail

Maps: 1. Mount Rogers National Recreation Area
2. USGS 7.5 minute quadrangle, Damascus, Va.
3. USGS 7.5 minute quadrangle, Abingdon, Va.
4. Guide to the Virginia Creeper Trail, available from the Virginia Creeper Trail Club, P.O. Box 2382, Abingdon, Va. 24212-2382
5. Mount Rogers National Recreation Area Trail Town Maps, Trail Guide to Beartree/ Damascus, Va., Area

Access: To reach the Damascus access, take U.S. 58 West from the intersection of U.S. 58 and Va. 91. Drive through the town of Damascus for 1.5 miles to the red caboose at the Virginia Creeper trailhead, located on the left just across Tennessee Laurel Creek. Park in the parking area.

Note: U.S. 58 makes several turns through Damascus; just follow the highway signs and make the appropriate turns.

To reach the Abingdon access, you can drive west on U.S. 58 into the quaint downtown section of the town. Travel to the traffic light marked Signal #3. You will see a sign for the Virginia Creeper Trail pointing left; turn left onto Pecan Street SE. The parking lot for the trailhead is on the right about 0.2 mile from Signal #3. The trail begins across the street. An old locomotive is on display at the trailhead.

If you are approaching Abingdon via Interstate 81, you can take Exit 19 from the north or Exit 17 from the south to reach the downtown section. From Exit 19, drive south on U.S.11 to Signal #3 and follow the directions described above. From Exit 17, turn left onto Cummings Street, travel to the traffic light marked Signal #2 and turn right onto Main Street. Go to Signal #3 and turn right, following the directions described above.

Elevation change: The elevation at Damascus is about 1,900 feet. You will pedal a slight descent for a few miles to a minimum of 1,750 feet at the confluence of the Middle and South Forks of the Holston River. The elevation then rises to about 2,050 feet by the end of the trail in Abingdon. The total elevation gain is about 300 feet; the total elevation loss is about 300 feet.

Configuration: One-way

The old Virginia-Carolina locomotive sits at the Abingdon trailhead.

T his route covers the western section of the Virginia Creeper Trail. The chapter describing the eastern half, which travels from Whitetop Gap to Damascus, will give you background about the Creeper's history as a railbed for the Virginia-Carolina Railroad and its current incarnation as a popular trail for cyclists, hikers, and horseback riders.

Like its eastern mate, this half of the Creeper is nontechnical and has a well-groomed surface of crushed stone. It is also an easy trail if pedaled as a one-way shuttle ride. However, if ridden as an out-and-back, this western section of the Creeper is a good bit easier than the eastern section. Its round-trip elevation gain is only 450 feet, which is quite a contrast to the 1,700 feet gained from Damascus to Whitetop Gap.

The scenery on the western section is also remarkably different from the eastern leg. Rather than running beside cascading white water, this section hugs the banks of the slowly flowing South Fork of the Holston River. You will cross 15 bridges and trestles, some over the river and others over deep, junglelike ravines. The highlight of the trail is the long trestle at the confluence of the South and Middle Forks of the Holston River. These two rivers meet to form South Holston Lake at this site.

The trail doesn't slice through any rocky gorges between Damascus and Abingdon, but it does flow past beautiful, rolling pastureland. Much of the ride passes through private land, including the "bull lot" that is filled with docile bulls who seem to care little about the strange-looking animals moving swiftly through their grazing land. Along the trail, there are several private gates you will have to stop, open, and pass through. Be sure to close them behind you. These private landowners have graciously allowed strangers access to their land. Repay their generosity with simple courtesy.

Along the route there are many log benches that are provided by the Virginia Creeper Trail Club. The members of this club are diligent watchdogs and trail advocates. You may see some of them emptying trash, erecting bulletin boards, repairing gates, or just chatting with tourists as you travel this trail.

0.0 Leave the town park in Damascus by pedaling across U.S. 58, away from the caboose.

1.3 Pedal across the paved Vail's Mill Road.

2.2 You will pass an old mill on the right. Across U.S. 58, there is a restaurant on the left.

3.2 The trail crosses the driveways in front of nearby houses.

3.4 Cross S.R. 1230.

4.5 You will pass under the U.S. 58 bridge and through a metal gate; be sure to close the gate behind you. You are entering the "bull lot" where you may see several large, but docile bulls.

5.2 This is a rough section of the trail; be careful.

5.5 You will ride next to what is locally called the "donkey pen" before crossing a paved road. You will see a metal bridge on the road to your right.

6.0 The trail passes through a gate; be sure to close the gate.

6.1 Pass through a metal gate. Keep closing those gates.

6.8 The trail crosses trestle #13.

6.9 The trail crosses a road at the Alvarado community. Alvarado Bible Church is on your left. This is the lowest point on the trail at 1,750 feet.

7.0 On the right is an old post office that was last used in 1956. It is now used as a store where you can purchase drinks and snacks.

8.2 The trail travels over the 526-foot-long trestle that spans this portion of South Holston Lake. This marks the confluence of the Middle and South Forks of the Holston River.

9.4 Cross trestle #8.

9.7 You will pedal through a gate and cross trestle #7.

9.8 Pass through gates at the Smith Farm. Be sure to close the gate behind you.

10.7 The trail crosses a very high trestle #6.

11.5 Cross trestle #5.

12.2 Cross Watauga Road before reaching the Watauga parking lot. You will pedal to the left of a permanent iron gate. Use caution, as this is a well-traveled road.

12.3 Cross the 480-foot-long trestle #4, which spans Fifteen Mile Creek.

12.9 Cross trestle #3, which crosses Berry Creek.

13.1 Cross trestle #2, which crosses Dry Branch.

14.9 You pedal over a golf-cart crossing and pass Winterham Estates, where you can see several luxury homes.

15.2 The trail crosses under an overpass on Interstate 81.

15.7 On the left is a park with benches and picnic tables. This was the site of the "Y" where steam engines made their turnaround.

16.0 You've reached the Abingdon trailhead for the Virginia Creeper Trail.

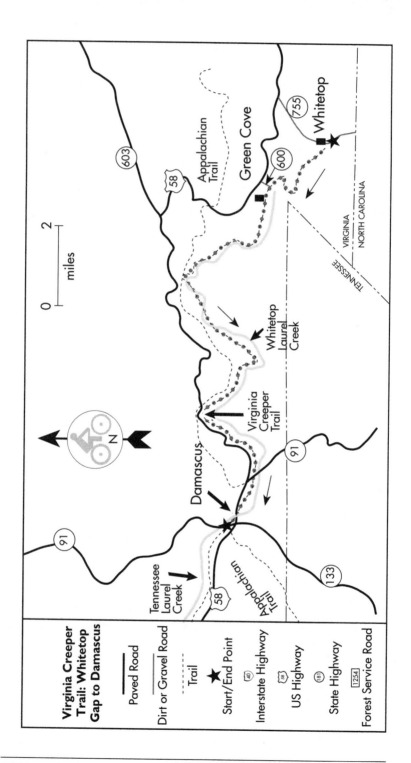

Virginia Creeper
Trail: Whitetop
Gap to Damascus

Paved Road

Dirt or Gravel Road

Trail

★ Start/End Point

40 Interstate Highway

58 US Highway

88 State Highway

1254 Forest Service Road

Whitetop

Green Cove

Appalachian Trail

Whitetop Laurel Creek

Virginia Creeper Trail

Damascus

Tennessee Laurel Creek

Appalachian Trail

VIRGINIA
NORTH CAROLINA

TENNESSEE

603

58

600

755

91

91

58

133

miles

0   2

N

Virginia Creeper Trail: Whitetop Gap to Damascus

Distance: 17.6 miles

Difficulty: Easy

Riding Surface: Rail trail

Maps: 1. Mount Rogers National Recreation Area
2. USGS 7.5 minute quadrangle, Konnarock, Va.
3. USGS 7.5 minute quadrangle, Damascus, Va.
4. USGS 7.5 minute quadrangle, Grayson, Va.-Tenn.-N.C.
5. Guide to the Virginia Creeper Trail, available from the Virginia Creeper Trail Club, P.O. Box 2382, Abingdon, Va. 24212-2382
6. Mount Rogers National Recreation Area Trail Town Maps, Trail Guide to Beartree/ Damascus, Va., Area

Access: To get to Whitetop Gap, there are two shuttle services available from Damascus. For a nominal fee, the Blue Blaze Bike & Shuttle (800-475-5095) and Mount Rogers Outfitters (800-337-5416) both provide quality shuttle service for you and your bike. Using one of these services saves time and reduces the traffic congestion at Whitetop Gap. You will also have an opportunity to learn about the history of the trail from the shuttle driver.

If you must drive, take U.S. 58 East from the intersection of U.S. 58 and Va. 91 near Damascus. Drive 9.7 miles to the intersection with Va. 603. Turn right to stay on U.S. 58 for 7 miles to Va. 726. Turn right onto Va. 726 and proceed 3 miles to the Whitetop Gap parking area. If you come to the Grayson County line, you went the wrong way.

To reach the Green Cove access, follow the above directions to the intersection of U.S. 58 and Va. 603. Turn right to stay on U.S. 58, then drive 4.2 miles to the turnoff for Green Cove Road (S.R. 600). Turn right onto Green Cove Road and drive 0.3 mile to the Green Cove Station, on the right. Park here to begin.

To reach the Damascus access, take U.S. 58 West from the intersection of U.S. 58 and Va. 91. Drive through the town of Damascus for 1.5 miles to the red caboose at the Virginia Creeper trailhead, located on the left just across Tennessee Laurel Creek. Park in the parking area. **Note:** U.S. 58 makes several turns through Damascus; just follow the highway signs and make the appropriate turns.

Elevation change: The ride begins at an elevation of 3,600 feet at Whitetop Gap and drops to 3,200 feet at Green Cove Station, then all the way to 2,400 feet at Taylors Valley and 1,900 feet at Damascus. There is no elevation gain on this section, when ridden east to west. The total elevation loss is 1,700 feet.

Configuration: One-way, if you use the shuttle service.

The Virginia Creeper Trail runs east to west for 33 miles from the Whitetop Mountain area to Abingdon, through some of the highest and most scenic terrain known to any rail trail.

The crushed-stone pathway is the abandoned railway corridor of the old Virginia-Carolina Railroad, known in former days as the "V-C." The first steam locomotive made its way from Abingdon to Damascus in February 1900. Later this backwoods railroad line was lengthened all the way to Elkland,

North Carolina. For many years, it was the only means of commercial transport from the high mountains to the valley towns of Abingdon and Damascus. Timber was hauled down from the mountains for processing in town, and occasionally, some of the mountain residents would hitch a ride on the train to and from the valley. These folks affectionately nicknamed the railroad "Virginia Creeper" for the slow crawl the locomotive made traveling west to east. Some people claim that the nickname also referred to the Virginia creeper vine growing near the tracks.

On March 31, 1977, the Virginia-Carolina Railroad made its last run. When the locomotive fell silent at the end of that historic day, some say the romance of the railroad era died. In the late 1950s, the Norfolk & Western Railroad Company presented the town of Abingdon with an old "V-C" steam locomotive for public display. It sits as a sentry at the trailhead in Abingdon and is a noble reminder of that period in American history.

You can see another remnant of this historical era at Green Cove Station, which is located three miles down the trail. There you can tour the original depot. Inside there are some signed photographs that were donated by O. Winston Link, a photographer who traveled through the area in the 1950s capturing the images of the old steam trains. One noticeable photograph is entitled "Maude Bows to the Virginia Creeper." From May to October, there is usually a forest-service volunteer at the station to answer questions.

At the starting point, you may want to take a brief side trip. If you turn right at the start of Whitetop Gap, it's only 0.1 mile to a nice view of a beaver pond on the left. You will also see several Christmas tree farms, since the elevation is perfect for growing the popular Fraser fir. To the north, you can glimpse the bald atop Whitetop Mountain.

Mile for mile, this trail is easy, though the distance can be taxing for some cyclists. If you set up a shuttle and ride east to west, you will pedal 17.5 easy miles. If you ride it as an out-and-back, the difficulty increases, due to the 1,700-foot elevation gain and the total distance of 35 miles. The surface of the trail consists of crushed rock and dirt and poses virtually no technical challenge. For the most part, it is well groomed, though you will find a few rocky stretches. Its gently descending grade, wide double track, smooth surface, and variety of ride options make the Virginia Creeper Trail an attractive mountain-bike ride for cyclists of diverse abilities.

The scenery on this eastern half of the trail is quite different from the section running from Damascus to Abingdon. The high-elevation hills play host to a variety of conifers not found at lower elevations. There is also a splash of high-elevation wildflowers, such as painted trillium, growing along this upper stretch of trail.

Several miles of this railway corridor plunge through Whitetop Laurel Gorge, leading cyclists past very old geologi-

A beaver dam under a trestle on the Virginia Creeper Trail

cal formations. Rock outcroppings dress the banks of Whitetop Laurel Creek to create exceptionally beautiful scenery. There are also dramatic views from some of the 31 trestles and bridges you will cross.

Note: The forest service recommends that you walk your bike across all trestles. It is also important for everyone's safety to remember to never get on a trestle when someone is crossing with a horse.

0.0   Start at the parking lot at Whitetop Station. Turn left, heading toward Green Cove. You cross the paved Whitetop Gap Road and continue straight. There is a sign that reads "Green Cove 3, Damascus 17."

0.1   Cross trestle # 46, which is very high. Get used to crossing these trestles, as you will cross several more.

2.9   Cross the paved road and walk across the newly restored bridge over Green Cove Creek. Directly across the road is Green Cove Station.

3.0   Arrive at Green Cove Station, which is the only remaining original depot on the Creeper Trail. The depot is left much the same as it was when the train used to come through here. Here you can find snacks, souvenirs, and the photographs described above. Public restrooms are located behind the depot, and there is a water fountain at the Green Cove Senior Center, next door to the depot.

5.4   Cross a dirt road at Callahan's Crossing. Continue straight on the trail. Green Cove Creek is now on the right and below you. There is a nice view of the rhododendron canopy below.

6.4   The Appalachian Trail joins the Creeper Trail from the right. Cross the double trestles at Creek Junction. To the left off the 563-foot second trestle is a nice view of

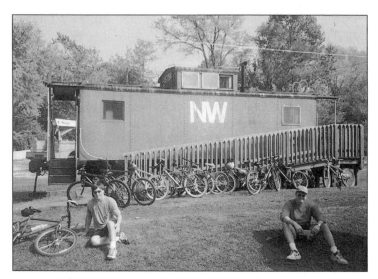
Red caboose in Damascus Town Park

the junction of Green Cove and Whitetop Creeks. There is a stone monument to Luther C. Hassinger at the end of the second trestle.

7.0   Continue straight at the Creek Junction parking lot.

7.1   The Appalachian Trail turns off to the right and heads into the forest. Double white blazes indicate a change in direction for the Appalachian Trail.

7.3   There are waterfalls on the right.

8.2   There are signs of beaver activity on the right for the next mile.

10.0   Cross trestle #28, which leads into Taylors Valley. A sign here shows the mileage to Straight Branch (3 miles) and Damascus (7 miles). On the right is gravel F.R. 49100. Continue on the Creeper Trail, the lower road on the right. The houses in Taylors Valley are private property.

10.2 Cross the gravel road. There is an old cabin on the left.

10.3 Go through the gate and cross the front yard of this residence. Make sure the gates are closed! If you have ridden on the New River Trail, you are aware of what can happen to the trail if this cooperative landowner becomes unhappy.

10.5 Walk across the trestle and close the gate.

10.8 Cross the paved road and enter Taylors Valley Picnic Area. There is a drink machine here. Pass the red caboose and re-enter the national-forest area.

13.0 The Straight Branch parking lot is on the right. Beech Grove Trail and the Appalachian Trail go off to the right.

13.9 There is a waterfall on the right.

15.0 You will cross an iron bridge.

16.1 The trail parallels U.S. 58 near the intersection with Va. 91.

16.2 The trail crosses Va. 91; exercise extreme caution on this very busy highway.

16.9 You will pedal across a paved road; U.S. 58 bends around to the right.

17.3 You will pedal across Shady Avenue.

17.5 Cross trestle #16 and enter Damascus Town Park.

17.6 Arrive at the red caboose in Damascus Town Park.

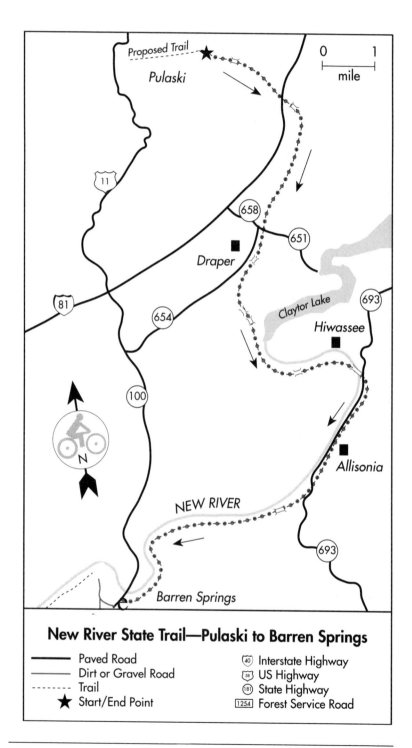

New River State Trail—Pulaski to Barren Springs

Paved Road
Dirt or Gravel Road
Trail
★ Start/End Point

⓪ Interstate Highway
Ⓢ US Highway
⑱ State Highway
1254 Forest Service Road

New River Trail: Pulaski to Barren Springs

Distance: 15.8 miles

Difficulty: Easy to moderate

Riding surface: Rail trail

Maps: 1. New River Trail State Park Trail Guide, available from New River Trail State Park, Route 2, Box 126F, Foster Falls, Va. 24360 (540-699-6778)
2. New River Trail State Park, available from Custom CAD Maps, Route 1, Box 117-A1, Draper, Va. 24324

Access: To reach the Pulaski access, take Exit 94 off I-81 and drive north on Va. 99 for 1.8 miles. Turn right onto Xaloy Way at the brown sign for New River Trail State Park's northern terminus. The parking area for the trail is on the right less than 0.1 mile from the turnoff. Do not park in the Xaloy plant's parking lot without permission.

Due to land disputes between mileposts 17 and 19, you cannot ride south past milepost 17 when coming from Pulaski. There is a route that uses state roads to circumvent the blocked section, but this 8-mile detour is not for inexperienced riders. This detour served as part of the route for the Tour DuPont—just to give you a proper perspective.

As a result of reported confrontations between bikers and residents living near the controversial section, most locals suggest that you avoid leaving the trail near the barricade. They advise riders to leave the trail at Allisonia. You can extend your ride southward from Allisonia, but turn around at the barricade and loop back to Allisonia for your southern exit. You can arrange shuttle services through the addresses listed at the end of this chapter.

The only other developed access point is located at Draper. From I-81, take Va. 658 east through Draper. Parking is available across from Bryson's Store, less than 1 mile from the interstate. You can also access at Hiwassee, but there is no developed parking area at this entrance. Horse trailers can park only at Draper.

Elevation change: The elevation at Pulaski is 1,900 feet. The ride climbs to 2,100 feet in the first 3 miles and then steadily drops for the next 7 miles until it reaches 1,850 feet. The rest of the ride is on a mostly level grade. The final elevation is 1,900 feet at Barren Springs. The total elevation gain is 250 feet.

If you ride this as an out-and-back from Pulaski, the greatest climb is on the return ride on a 2-mile stretch near Draper. The elevation climbs from 1,850 feet to 2,100 feet in this section.

Configuration: One-way

In the late 1800s, the most common sounds along this path were probably the wail of train whistles and the hiss of steam locomotives as they chugged along the steel rails once embedded in this track.

These beautiful miles of trail threading through the rolling green hills of southwest Virginia were once part of the railroad right of way used by the Norfolk & Western Railroad Company. Lead, iron, copper, and other minerals were in rich supply in this part of the country. As a result, mining flourished here, and many manufacturing companies sprang up. The railroad was constructed to service this thriving industry, transporting the mining spoils from the hills of Virginia to the rest of America. People looking for work moved into the area, and towns were born along the rail line, many of which are still in

Expansive views of the New River are best appreciated from the bridges.

existence today. Though the times were tough and the days long and hard, the mining business of southwest Virginia prospered.

Today, the locomotives are history and the old crossties have been removed, leaving only the memories of a bygone era. This abandoned railway corridor is one of America's popular rail trails, part of a recent movement to utilize old railroad rights of way as parks for public recreation. New River Trail is Virginia's only totally linear state park, or greenway. It is a multiuse trail, with all but two of its 57 miles now open to the public. The result is a happy mingling of bicyclists, hikers, and equestrians. Most of the trail work was done by volunteers, so if you run into one, be sure to give him or her a grateful pat on the back.

The trail is not technically challenging, but you *will* need a mountain bike or, at the very least, an all-terrain bicycle. Forget the skinny-tired bikes that work so well on pavement. You will need fat, knobby tires for the loose gravel and for rolling over rocks.

You will sometimes coast or pedal easily through splendid

Virginia hill country. Rolling farmland dotted with cattle, beautiful green hills, and wildflower-filled meadows will envelop you along some sections. Other sections offer a striking contrast, with sheer rock walls soaring high above the trail on one side and the shimmering water of the New River placidly drifting by on the other. Tall grasses bend in the gentle breezes, and handfuls of brightly colored wildflowers push up through the moist soil to drink in the mild sunshine.

Thirty-nine miles of the New River Trail hug the banks of the river, creating an especially scenic mountain-bike ride. Not only will you pedal beside this, the second-oldest river in the world, but you will also pedal over it. In the northern section of the trail, there are nine bridges and trestles, some of which offer incredibly expansive views.

Note: Notice that the mileages noted here are two miles less than the mileages noted on the milepost markers along the trail. This is because your ride begins two miles past milepost marker #1.

0.0 The ride begins from the Pulaski parking area.

0.4 You will pedal across a wooden trestle over Peak Creek. A nearby geological survey marker indicates you are 1,933 feet above sea level.

0.8 A private road crosses the trail.

1.0 You will pass milepost marker #3. This is the first milepost on the trail.

1.4 A private access road crosses the trail.

1.6 You will pass under I-81.

1.9 You will pedal across the wooden McAdam Trestle. Draper Mountain is to the west. You can see several towers atop Peak's Knob, which stands at 3,332 feet.

2.0 You will pass milepost marker #4.

2.6 This is the top of the grade from Pulaski, known locally as "The Hump." A small shelter with tables is located here.

2.7 A private road crosses the trail.

3.0 You will pass milepost marker #5.

4.0 You will pass milepost marker #6.

4.2 This is the Draper access point. New River Bicycles is located nearby; here, you can arrange some bike repairs or buy parts and accessories. You can also get food and camping supplies at a nearby grocery store. There is also a portable toilet here.

4.6 You will pedal across a long wooden trestle over Sloan Branch.

4.8 You will pedal across a gravel drive about 20 feet from a paved road.

5.3 A private road crosses the trail.

5.8 You will pedal across a wooden trestle over a stream and S.R. 658.

6.0 You will pedal across the highest wooden trestle on the trail. This trestle crosses a small bay of Claytor Lake.

7.0 You will pedal across a wooden trestle; some homes are on the right.

7.1 A trestle crosses a small stream in Dog Bite Hollow.

8.0 You will pass milepost marker #10.

8.3   You will pedal across the 951-foot Hiwassee Trestle, which crosses Claytor Lake.

8.5   You will pedal across S.R. 693 in Hiwassee.

9.5   You will pedal across a private road. This road leads to a mine where pigment is mined for paint. The locals refer to the area as "paint rocks" or "paint banks."

10.2   You will see the entrance to the boat ramp and parking area for Claytor Lake.

10.6   You will see the community of Allisonia. The Allisonia Methodist Church, which was built in 1891, is east of the trail. The railroad station is located on the lake side. You can arrange canoe and bike rentals or shuttle services at Allisonia Trading Post, which is located here. This is the recommended exit location. If you proceed

Expect to pass some horses on the New River Trail.

to the barricade, turn around and come back to this location to exit.

10.8   You will pedal across S.R. 693.

11.2   Just after passing milepost marker #13, you will see a cable-car system going over the river to a gauging station on the opposite bank. Years ago, the gauging station operator would climb into a cable car and scoot along a cable strung across the river. At the center of the river, he would lower a weighted measuring cord into the water to obtain the river's depth.

11.4   You will pedal across the 405-foot Big Reed Island Creek Trestle.

12.1   A waterfall is on the left. Milepost marker #14 is nearby.

13.6   There is a shelter with a table here.

14.0   You will pass milepost marker #16.

15.4   You will see high cliffs, which the locals call the "palisades of the New River."

15.6   Turn around at the S.R. 100 bridge.

Note: If you would like to arrange shuttle service, bike rentals, or other trail-related services at the Draper access, contact Lanny Sparks, New River Bicycles, Ltd., Route 1, Box 175, Draper, Va. 24324 (540-980-1741). At Allisonia, you can arrange these services through Allisonia Trading Post, HC02 Box 15B, Allisonia, VA 24347 (540-980-2051). At Foster Falls, you can contact New River Adventures at their Wytheville office at 1007 North 4th Street, Wytheville, VA 24382 (540-228-8311). New River Adventures was granted the New River Trail State Park concessions that are actually at Foster Falls.

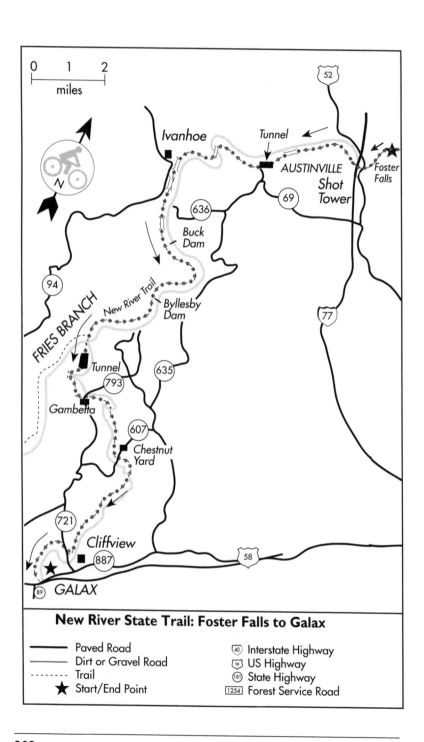

New River State Trail: Foster Falls to Galax

——— Paved Road	⑩	Interstate Highway
——— Dirt or Gravel Road	🛡	US Highway
- - - - Trail	⑱	State Highway
★ Start/End Point	1254	Forest Service Road

New River Trail:
Foster Falls to Galax

Distance: 29.1 miles

Difficulty: Easy to moderate

Riding surface: Rail trail

Maps: 1. New River Trail State Park Trail Guide, available from New River Trail State Park, Route 2, Box 126F, Foster Falls, VA 24360 (540-699-6778)
2. New River Trail State Park, available from Custom CAD Maps, Route 1, Box 117-A1, Draper, Va. 24324

Access: To reach Foster Falls, which is now the location of the administrative offices of the New River Trail, take Va. 52 to S.R. 608 (Foster Falls Road) and go east, following the park signs.

To reach the Galax access, take Exit 14 off I-77. Drive west on U.S. 58 for 10 miles; you will pass through the town of Galax. The parking area for the trail is well marked. It is located on the right just past Chestnut Creek.

Note: There are additional access points south of Foster Falls. The other developed access points are located at Buck Dam, Byllesby Dam, Ivanhoe, Gambetta, Chestnut Yard, and Cliffview. There are horse- and bike-rental outfits at Cliffview. You can rent canoes, bikes, and inner tubes at Foster Falls. An undeveloped access point is located at Austinville. All of these access points were train stops during railroad days.

Due to ongoing litigation with an area landowner, there is a 2-mile section of the trail that is closed from mileposts 17 to 19 (Barren Springs to Lone Ash). To extend your ride, you can add a 10-mile loop by riding north from Foster Falls to milepost 19 at Lone Ash. This loop offers the scenic river on one side, interesting cliffs on the other.

Elevation change: The elevation at Shot Tower is 1,950 feet. The ride gradually climbs over the next 29 miles to a maximum 2,350 feet. The total elevation gain is 400 feet. Riding this trail in the opposite direction—from south to north, or from Galax to Foster Falls—is an even easier route, with an elevation *loss* of 400 feet.

Configuration: One-way

This segment of the New River Trail is loaded with historical sites. Historic Foster Falls Village, where this route begins, now serves as the park's headquarters and significant recreation area. The village dates to the mid- and late-1800s and features a railroad depot, hotel, saw-and-gristmill, iron furnace, and numerous associated buildings. The state is turning the surrounding 160 acres into a state park featuring whitewater rafting, bicycling, fishing, horseback riding, and camping.

Foster Falls, which is part of the New River Trail State Park, already serves as a major recreation area for the park, with both trail and river access. Here you can find two canoe/small-boat launches, a picnic shelter, and canoe, bicycle, and inner-tube rentals.

Just south of Foster Falls is Shot Tower Historical State Park. In 1807, Englishman Thomas Jackson probably never dreamed that the shot tower he built would be designated a National Historic Mechanical Engineering Landmark almost 200 years later. This 75-foot-high stone tower was built on a bluff, with a 75-foot-deep shaft below the structure. Crude wooden stairs

Shot Tower

led up to the top level, which contained a fireplace and a chimney. It was here that slaves placed lead in a kettle, melted it, and then poured it through sieves. The molten lead fell 150 feet from the top of the tower to a kettle of water waiting on the floor of the shaft. This distance of 150 feet supposedly ensured the uniform roundness of the shot. The shot was later retrieved from the kettle through an access tunnel that connected the New River and the shaft. You'll find restrooms and water here, and for a small fee, you can climb to the top of the tower for an impressive view of the surrounding countryside.

The historical highlights along this rail trail are not concentrated simply around Shot Tower and Foster Falls. One of the first points of interest you will reach as you pedal south toward Galax is the town of Austinville. General Andrew Lewis, Daniel Boone, and many other colonial frontiersmen reportedly stopped at Austinville, known then as the "Lead Mines." It was in this small mining town that the Fincastle Resolutions, a precursor of the Declaration of Independence, were written.

The mining of lead was a thriving industry that began in the late 1700s. Austinville was the site of a number of mines. The lead deposits were discovered when Colonel Robert

Chiswell was hiding in a small cave during an Indian raid. His land was confiscated during the Revolutionary War because he sided with the English.

At the time of the Civil War, the mines were incorporated and consolidated as the Wythe Union Lead Mine Company. Its name notwithstanding, the company was the chief supplier of lead to the Confederate troops. The name didn't fool the Yankees, as the company was attacked twice during the war. The mine now lays claim to being the site of the oldest continuously operated mine in North America.

Before you pedal away from Austinville, you might want to stop by the Austin Homestead, the home of Moses Austin, who gave the town its name. This man owned the local lead mines and was the father of Stephen F. Austin, the "Father of Texas." It is believed that Stephen Austin was born in this old house near the slowly rolling waters of the New River.

Just like the northern half of the New River Trail, this ride is relatively easy. There are no screaming descents, no challenging climbs, and no technical single-track sections that dangle you from 1,000-foot cliffs. What you will find as you spin down the trail is a peaceful ride set in exceptionally beautiful backwoods country. The trail is wide and has a nontechnical surface of crushed rock. You might even see some cinders on this old railroad bed, leftovers from the coal burned to power the steam locomotives. Most sections are smooth and well groomed, though there are a few bumpy areas where horse hooves have made deep indentations in the soft soil.

Most of the trail parrots the moves of the New River and Chestnut Creek, slowly winding through the gaps and saddles of the mountains. In some sections, you will pedal next to calm, clear water that seems to barely flow. In other sections, the pulse of the river quickens to frothy, thundering rapids. You will cross the river and creek several times on the southern half of the trail via sturdy bridges and restored trestles. Some are short and hover only a few feet above the water, while others are long and high. Though these bridges might give some folks heart palpitations, the vistas offered from their heights are truly stunning.

If all of this isn't enough, how does pedaling blindly through a dark, damp stone tunnel grab you? The trail disappears into two tunnels, one of which is particularly memorable as it curves for 193 feet through cold, wet, pitch-dark blackness. As you approach this tunnel, try to imagine its construction back in the late 1800s. Workmen had the benefit of only crude tools and dynamite to barrel a path through the mountain. The temperature inside the tunnel is dramatically cooler than outside. Most of the time, icy droplets of water drip from crevices in the stone. Pedaling past the mouth of the tunnel and into the dark cavern, you might experience for a moment what Jonah must have felt in the belly of the great fish. But in no time, the tunnel spits you back into a sun-drenched world that will have you squinting as your eyes try to adjust to the light.

As you move down the trail, you will spin through a beautiful forest of mixed hardwoods, pines, hemlocks, and rhododendron. In the spring, you will pedal deep into a world of pastel colors, as blooming dogwoods brighten the high ridges and wildflowers dot the newly green riverbanks like pale yellow and lavender Easter eggs. Summertime rides are generally comfortable, due to the canopy of shade offered by mature oaks

Buck Dam

and other hardwoods. This same deciduous forest promises a vibrant show of color in autumn, when the hills of Virginia seem to catch on fire.

0.0   From the parking area at Foster Falls Station, pedal south on the trail, heading toward the Shot Tower and I-77. The Foster Falls Forge and Furnace is located across from the station. It was constructed in 1881 and produced 6.75 tons of iron daily.

0.3   You will pedal past the old train station and several buildings that are being restored. You will see an outfitter's building on the right. On the left is a brick building that used to house the Fosters Falls Orphanage and Children's Home. Plans call for converting this building to a bed-and-breakfast inn.

0.4   You will see a farm road to the left that leads to the Neuhoff-Jones farm. Until the state purchased the land between the trail and the river in 1995, this section of the trail was closed.

0.7   You will see milepost marker #24. You can also see the upper rapids of Foster Falls.

0.8   In the river, you can see the remains of the 1887 trestle, which was destroyed in the 1916 flood.

1.7   You will cross Shorts Creek Trestle, which crosses over U.S. 52 and Shorts Creek.

1.9   There is an access trail to Shot Tower on the left. At one point on this road, it will look like you are on a driveway to a farmhouse. Continue up the hill, and you will see the parking area for Shot Tower on the right.

2.0   A hikers-only access trail to Shot Tower is on the left.

The longer of the two tunnels on the New River Trail State Park.

2.1   You will pass under the bridge carrying I-77 over the New River.

3.8   There is a trail bench at milepost marker #27. The Shot Tower Rapids are on the right.

4.5   You will pedal across the Indian Branch Trestle.

4.6   A shelter and picnic table are on the left.

5.2   You will cycle through the 135-foot New River Tunnel.

5.6   You will cross S.R. 69. This is a busy highway which provides access to the northern part of Austinville. On the right you will see Lead Mines Bridge. A grocery/ hardware store and restaurant are located across the bridge to the left on S.R. 619.

6.0   You will pass the site of Lead Mines. The trail skirts an abandoned industrial area. Warning signs advise trail users not to stray from the trail, due to the hazardous nature of this industrial area.

6.7   Across the river from milepost marker #30, you can see the mouth of Cripple Creek.

7.0   The 670-foot Ivanhoe Trestle crosses the New River.

8.3   The Ivanhoe parking lot is on the right. You will notice a large object to the side of this large parking area. This was supposedly a stone crusher. This community was known as Brown Hill because of its ore deposits until the wife of the owner of the local furnace read Sir Walter Scott's *Ivanhoe*.

8.4   A trestle crosses a stream and S.R. 639.

8.9   You will cross a stream and S.R. 743.

9.7   S.R. 764, which used to provide access to National Carbide Company's Ivanhoe plant, enters here. Do not enter the industrial site because of hazardous waste.

10.1 S.R. 764 crosses under the trail. S.R. 758 then crosses the trail. Steel gates on both sides of this road limit vehicle access to the trail. You will also see milepost marker #33.

11.0 You will cross a wooden trestle. Big Branch enters the New River at this point.

11.9 You will reach Buck Dam. This dam was built by the Appalachian Power Company. The Cliff Trail, an old wagon road that parallels the New River Trail, begins here. The Cliff Trail rejoins the New River Trail at Ivanhoe.

12.8 You will see a sign identifying Ruth's Spring on the right. This is an unapproved spring. There is also a trail shelter nearby.

13.2 S.R. 737 crosses the trail.

14.4 Byllesby Dam is on the left. You will pedal across Byllesby Road (S.R. 602). This dam and Buck Dam were both built in 1913 for the Appalachian Power Company. Materials were brought in by rail because of the lack of roads in the area. You can also see an abandoned passenger stop and a former damkeeper's house on the property.

15.9 A trail shelter and picnic table are on your left.

16.5 You will pedal across a wooden trestle over Brush Creek. A portable toilet and picnic tables are on the right.

17.1 Fries Branch Trail leaves the main trail and branches off to the right. Picnic tables and a shelter are located at this trail junction. Stay on the main trail. You will pedal across the 1,089-foot Fries Junction Trestle over the New River. Chestnut Creek merges into the New River at this point.

17.7 You will pedal through the 193-foot Chestnut Creek Tunnel, the longer of the two tunnels on the trail. Chestnut Creek is on your left.

19.5 You will cross S.R. 793 at Gambetta Crossing. This is one of the developed access points along the trail. Just past the road, you will pedal across a wooden trestle over the creek.

22.6 You will cross S.R. 607 at Chestnut Yard; a shelter is located here.

23.4 You will pedal across a short wooden trestle.

23.6 You will pedal across a bridge; Chestnut Creek Falls are located east of the bridge. Just before the bridge is a trail shelter.

24.4 This is the site of Iron Mines Junction, where extensive open-pit and shaft iron mining took place. The ridges have been retimbered recently.

26.8 The Cliffview access is here. You will pedal across a busy road (S.R. 721). A convenience store and facilities for horse and bicycle rental are located at this trail access. The ranger station with public restrooms and safe water is located to the south of the road. The Cliffside Manor is located to the west of the trail. One of the manor's previous owners was T.L. Felts, the owner of the Baldwin-Felts Detective Agency. It was this agency that supplied mine guards to the coal companies of central Appalachia during the violent labor struggles that took place in the early twentieth century. The John Sayles movie, *Matewan*, dealt with these struggles.

28.5 You will pedal across a wooden trestle over Chestnut Creek and then pedal across a road.

28.7 There is a trail shelter here.

29.1 Begin cycling from the Galax parking area. You will see a trail shelter.

Note: There are many different ways to cycle this half of the New River Trail. The easiest way to pedal these 29 miles is to leave a vehicle at Foster Falls parking area and begin riding in Galax. It's all downhill.

If you want to pedal this half of the trail as an out-and-back ride, you will probably want to begin at Foster Falls so that you can get the (easy) climbing out of the way in the first half of the ride. The total distance is then a little over 58 miles.

There are two outfitters near the Foster Falls parking area that offer supplies and rentals:

Cherry Creek Cyclery & More
Route 2, Box 110
Foster Falls, VA 24360
Phone/Fax: 540-699-2385

New River Adventures
1007 North 4th Street
Wytheville, VA 24382
Phone: 540-228-8311

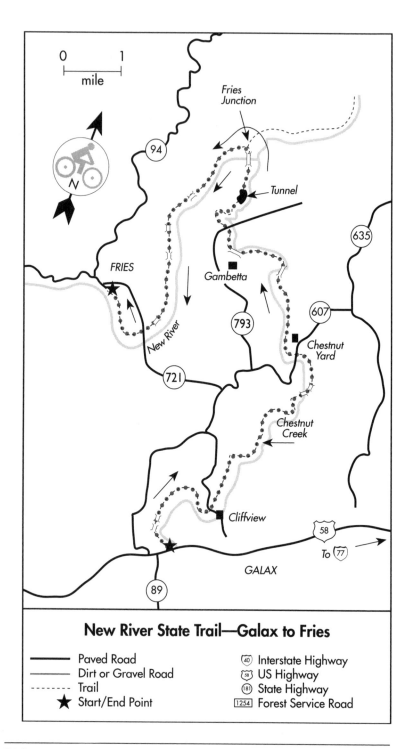

New River State Trail—Galax to Fries

———— Paved Road	⑩ Interstate Highway
———— Dirt or Gravel Road	⑤⑧ US Highway
- - - - - Trail	⑱ State Highway
★ Start/End Point	⒧⒉⒌⒋ Forest Service Road

New River Trail: Galax to Fries

Distance: 17.5 miles

Difficulty: Easy to moderate

Riding surface: Rail trail

Maps: 1. New River Trail State Park Trail Guide, available from New River Trail State Park, Route 2, Box 126F, Foster Falls, VA 24360 (540-699-6778)
  2. New River Trail State Park, available from Custom CAD Maps, Route 1, Box 117-A1, Draper, Va. 24324

Access: To reach the Galax access, take Exit 14 off I-77. Drive west on U.S. 58 for 10 miles; you will pass through the town of Galax. The parking area for the trail is well marked. It is located on the right just past Chestnut Creek.

To reach the Fries Branch access, begin at the intersection of U.S. 58/U.S. 221 and N.C. 94 and follow N.C. 94 for approximately 4.5 miles to the town of Fries (pronounced freeze). The parking area for the New River Trail is located at the town park and caboose.

Note: There are additional access points in this section. The other developed access points are at Cliffview, Chestnut Yard, and Gambetta. All of these were former train stops during railroad days.

Elevation change: The ride begins at an elevation of 2,350 feet in Galax and drops to 2,100 feet at the Fries Branch junction. It then climbs to 2,150 feet at the Fries terminus. The total elevation gain on this one-way stretch is only 50 feet, but if you make this an out-and-back ride from Galax to Fries to Galax, the total elevation gain is 300 feet.

Configuration: One-way

The beauty of a rail trail like the New River Trail is its appeal to almost any type of bicyclist. You don't have to be an expert mountain-bike racer to fully appreciate all this trail has to offer. Any cyclist—including beginners, children, senior citizens, and occasional cyclists—will find this trail easy when pedaled in part. And because of its impressive one-way length, stronger cyclists also enjoy the New River Trail. Many experienced riders find that it offers an appealing change of pace from the rough-and-tumble world of challenging single track. The trail also offers a long, steady workout unbroken by traffic and trail obstacles.

This trail is actually an abandoned rail corridor once used by the Norfolk & Western Railroad Company. The right of way was donated to the state of Virginia for use as a park and has now been restored to become the state's first linear park. Fifty-seven miles of trail stretch from Pulaski to Galax, with a short southwestern leg branching off to the town of Fries. Most of the 57 miles are open to the public and are heavily used by cyclists, hikers, joggers, horseback riders, and even cross-country skiers.

This particular ride from Galax to Fries follows a wide double-track trail with a smooth crushed-rock surface. Horses have created some rutted areas in a few sections, though these bumpy spots can be easily negotiated. You might expect to find crowds of trail users on this popular path, but the long length tends to spread folks out. The closer you are to a major access point, though, the greater the number of people you will pass.

As you pedal, you will be flanked by beautiful pastoral scen-

The trail closely parallels the New River.

ery. The trail meanders past rolling green farmland and visits grazing cattle, who occasionally lift their heads to study passing cyclists. For almost its entire 17.5 miles, the trail parallels the sparkling waters of Chestnut Creek and the New River. Because of the slow-moving water in most sections of the New River, this is a popular destination for canoeists wishing to pole, rather than paddle, their way through its shallow waters.

A fatal train wreck occurred in 1928 near the junction of the New River and Chestnut Creek. A passenger train backing into Fries was struck by a freight train leaving town nearly 30 minutes behind schedule. Apparently, the freight train was traveling so fast that it split the end coach of the passenger train completely in half. It is said that the wooden car burst apart like a split melon, leaving the two sides lying on opposite sides of the track.

Note: Cherry Creek Cyclery & More has a good website (www.cccyclery.com) for information about the New River Trail.

0.0   Begin cycling from the Galax parking area.

0.5   You will cross a wooden trestle over Chestnut Creek and then pedal across a road. There is a trail shelter here.

0.6   You will pedal across a wooden trestle.

2.3   The Cliffview access is here. You will pedal across a busy road (S.R. 721). A convenience store and facilities for horse and bicycle rental are located at this trail access. The ranger station with public restrooms and safe water is located to the south of the road. The Cliffside Manor is located to the west of the trail. One of the manor's previous owners was T.L. Felts, the owner of the Baldwin-Felts Detective Agency. It was this agency that supplied mine guards to the coal companies of central Appalachia during the violent labor struggles that took place in the early twentieth century. The John Sayles movie, *Matewan*, dealt with these struggles.

4.7   This is the site of Iron Mines Junction, where extensive open-pit and shaft iron mining took place. The ridges have recently been retimbered.

5.5   You will pedal across a bridge; Chestnut Creek Falls are located east of the bridge. Just past the bridge is a trail shelter.

5.7   You will pedal across a short wooden trestle.

6.5   You will cross S.R. 607 at Chestnut Yard; a shelter is located here.

8.5   You will pedal across a wooden trestle over the creek.

9.6   You will pedal across a wooden trestle over a creek. S.R. 793 intersects the trail here at Gambetta Crossing. This is one of the developed access points along the trail.

11.4 You will pedal through the 193-foot Chestnut Creek Tunnel. This is the longest of the two tunnels on the New River Trail.

12.0 You will pedal over the New River on the 1,089-foot Fries Junction Trestle. Chestnut Creek merges into the New River at this point.

12.2 After crossing the trestle, turn left. This section of the trail takes you to the community of Fries.

12.5 You will cross a wooden trestle.

13.1 You can see the lower shoals of Double Shoals.

13.7 You will pedal across a wooden trestle.

14.3 You will cross another wooden trestle. There is also a good view of the upper shoals of Double Shoals.

14.8 You will cross yet another wooden trestle.

Horses can be rented at the Cliffview access.

15.6 You will see the Low Water Bridge on the left. The bridge gets its name because it is lower than the average annual flood level of the river. You will cross S.R. 721. A convenience store is located at this intersection. A telephone is located at the store.

15.9 You will cross a wooden trestle.

16.4 You will cross a dirt road.

17.2 You will pedal across a wooden trestle.

17.5 You will arrive at the Fries Branch access. Fries was developed as a company town by Colonel F. H. Fries for his cotton mill. Fries built a dam on the New River in 1903 to provide power for his mill. The mill is currently closed.

Index